SpringerBriefs in Computer Science

More information about this series at http://www.springer.com/series/10028

Joakim Kävrestad

Guide to Digital Forensics

A Concise and Practical Introduction

 Springer

Joakim Kävrestad
University of Skövde
Skövde
Sweden

ISSN 2191-5768   ISSN 2191-5776   (electronic)
SpringerBriefs in Computer Science
ISBN 978-3-319-67449-0   ISBN 978-3-319-67450-6   (eBook)
https://doi.org/10.1007/978-3-319-67450-6

Library of Congress Control Number: 2017952933

Printed on acid-free paper

This Springer imprint is published by Springer Nature
The registered company is Springer International Publishing AG
The registered company address is: Gewerbestrasse 11, 6330 Cham, Switzerland

Preface

This book introduces the reader to the world of digital forensics in a practical and accessible manner. The book was written to fulfill the need for a book that introduces forensic methodology and sound forensic thinking combined with hands-on examples for common tasks in a computer forensic examination. The author of this book has several years of experience as a computer forensic examiner, and is now working as a university-level lecturer. To further ensure that the content provided in this book is relevant and accurate in the real world, Jan-Åke Pettersson from the Swedish Police were asked to provide a feedback on the content. Thank you ever so much for your help!

This book is intended for students that are looking for an introduction to computer forensics and can also be used as a collection of instructions for practitioners. The aim is to describe and explain the steps taken during a forensic examination with the intent of making the reader aware of the constraints and considerations that apply during a forensic examination in law enforcement and in the private sector. Upon reading this book, the reader should have a proper overview of the field of digital forensics and started a journey of becoming a computer forensic expert!

Skövde, Sweden   Joakim Kävrestad

Contents

Introduction

This is a book written for the sole reason that when I wanted to hold a course on digital forensics, I could not find a textbook that seemed to fulfill my requirements. What I needed a book to cover were the following:

- Sound forensic thinking and methodology
- A discussion on what Computer Forensics can assist with
- Hands-on examples

My answer to my own needs was, well, to write my own book. It has become obvious to me that writing a book that fulfills those demands is not a very easy task. The main problem lies within making proper hands-on examples. For that reason I decided to put an emphasis on what digital forensics is at its very core and to make this piece of literature relevant worldwide, I have tried to omit everything that only seems relevant in a certain legislation. That being said, this is the book for you if you want to get an introduction to what computer forensics is, what it can do, and of course what it cannot do. It did feel good to use some sort of well-known forensic software for the examples in this book. I decided to go with the AccessData Forensic Toolkit for the sole reason that AccessData provides the ability to get certified, free of charge, at the time of writing.

This book begins with setting the stage for forensics examinations by discussing the theoretical foundation that the author seems as relevant and important for the area. The book will then take a more practical approach and discuss how's and why's about some key forensic concepts. Finally, the book will provide a section with information on how to find and interpret several artifacts. It should at this point be noticed that the book does not, by far, cover every single case, question, or artifact. The practical examples are rather here to serve as demonstrations of how to implement a forensically sound way of examining digital evidence. Throughout the book you will find real-world examples where I provide examples on when something was used or important in a real-world setting.

Since most computers targeted for a forensic examination is running some version of Windows, the examples and demonstrations in this book are presented in a Windows environment. Being the most recent flavor of Windows, Windows 10 was used. However, the information should to a very large extent be applicable for previous version of Windows.

Also, every chapter in the book comes with a "Questions and tasks" section. The answers to the questions or tasks are located in Appendix A—solutions.

Happy reading!

Part I
Theory

Now that the book kept you interested this far it is time to discuss what digital forensics actually is. This will be done in a very theoretical manner, but I have tried to keep it short. This part begins with an overview of what digital forensics and cybercrime is, before discussing some computer theory that is necessary for a forensic examiner to be familiar with. The final chapters will discuss how to collect digital evidence in a structured manner, how to analyze digital information, and write forensic reports.

Chapter 1
What Is Digital Forensics?

Abstract This chapter introduces the concept of digital forensics and provides a discussion of what computer forensics is, examining data in order to reconstruct what happened in a digital environment. Further, the chapter discusses the steps involved in a forensic examination in a digital environment, from collecting evidence to reporting on the findings of the examination. Common constraints and processes handled during a forensics examination are also introduced. Emphasis is put on making the reader understand the reason for a computer forensic examination and the fact that computer forensics follows the same rules and regulations as traditional forensic disciplines. The fact that a forensic examination is commonly initiated for a reason, answering some question, is also described. The aim of the chapter is to provide the reader with a brief and nontechnical overview of the subject digital forensics. As such, the chapter can be read and understood without any technical knowledge.

Keywords Digital forensics · Definition · Forensic process

So then, what is Digital Forensics? Well, the most simple of explanations could be that it is the examination of digital storage and environments in order to determine what has happened. "What has happened", in this context could be whether or not a crime was committed, whether or not someone remote controlled a certain computer, when a picture was taken or if a computer was subject to intrusion? That being said, it can be basically anything.

However, looking at some forensic investigations it is evident that saying "What has happened" is not covering the entire field of computer forensics since forensic examiners also look into what is currently happening. There has, for instance been several cases in Sweden, and globally, were forensic examiners monitored network traffic in order to capture data that was later used to identify sexual predators. There are also situations when forensic examiners, during house searches, record what is currently happening on a computer.

© The Author(s) 2017
J. Kävrestad, *Guide to Digital Forensics*, SpringerBriefs in Computer Science,
https://doi.org/10.1007/978-3-319-67450-6_1

Looking to the scientific community, Reith et al. (2002) described digital forensics in the following way:

> Digital forensics is a relatively new science. Derived as a synonym for computer forensics, its definition has expanded to include the forensics of all digital technology. Whereas computer forensics is defined as "the collection of techniques and tools used to find evidence in a computer

Today, this definition seems a bit old but it does hold a few key aspects. To begin with, they describe that computer forensics is a collection of techniques and tools. While those are definatly two important aspects, this definition does not fit my personal beliefs as it kind of omits the methodology and mindset that, for me, is the foundation of digital forensics. However, it does capture that digital forensics extends to all digital technology and that is an important aspect as today, important evidence may be found in everything from thumb drives to computers or the cloud.

A more recent description is found on www.forensiccontrol.com (2017):

> Computer forensics is the practice of collecting, analyzing and reporting on digital data in a way that is legally admissible. It can be used in the detection and prevention of crime and in any dispute where evidence is stored digitally. Computer forensics follows a similar process to other forensic disciplines, and faces similar issues.

What is noticeable in this description is that it determines the tasks involved during a forensic investigation; collecting, analyzing, and reporting. It also describes that computer forensics is comparable to other forensic disciplines and that does suggest that methods used and conclusions drawn during a computer forensic investigation should face the same scrutiny as an analysis of a fingerprint or DNA test. The rest of section will discuss each of these, beginning with establishing a model that could be used to describe a digital forensic examination.

1.1 A Forensic Examination

As we just established, the foundation of digital forensics is that it is the practice of collecting, analyzing, and reporting on digital data. It does, for sure, also impose that there is some data that we target for examination and a reason for the examination. It does also impose that, unless we do the examination for the fun of it, there is someone that we should report back to. I have collected those aspects and formed the very abstract model shown in Fig. 1.1 that does try to summarize the named aspects in a graphical way.

Figure 1.1 reflects the discussed processes and the inputs or outputs that should be present in each process. From top to bottom *Collect* should be the process of collecting digital evidence. I would also say that in this process you do target a person or a data source that would commonly be a device.

Having a person as a target would be the normal state in a criminal investigation where you have someone that is suspected of a crime. You would then, after getting a search warrant, start searching for devices that belongs to the suspect. In a

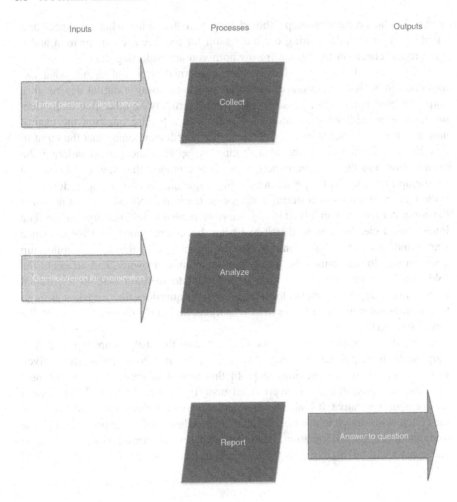

Fig. 1.1 Overview of forensic processes

corporate setting it could be more common to target a device rather a person, it would all depend on the reason for doing the investigation.

In this process, it is important to mention that in order to collect the correct data you need a proper order. The order in this case would include the target person or devices to collect data from but it should also include the reason for the investigation, at least on an abstract level. This is because you would look for vastly different data sources if you are investigating a suspected malware attack of a child abuse case. It is also important to know if you should prepare to collect information from volatile data sources such as memory circuits or only need to care about static media such as hard drives. Another technical consideration is if you should expect encrypted data or not. While there will be a more detailed technical discussion on data collection later in this book, it is important to mention that you need to come prepared. The preparation steps should help you determine what to expect and should at least include figuring out the reason for the forensic examination and a background check on the person from whom you are collecting data.

The process of *Analyzing* data is more concerned with finding out what has happened in a digital environment or what was done using a digital device. In a corporate environment, a forensic expert would normally be quite free to conduct whatever examinations she wants. However, with a precise question the examination will without doubt be more efficient. It is worth mentioning that the input to this phase is commonly found in a discussion between the person ordering the examination and the forensic expert. Also, it is common that new questions and follow-up questions will arise during the investigation. As one example, during an investigation of a computer during a drug case the initial request was to find out if the computer had been involved in any activities related to selling drugs online. The investigation clearly showed that it had been, but a large portion of the evidence was found in folders shared among several computers. In this case, a follow-up question was to determine who, more than the computer owner, had access to the folders in question. As a final note it important to mention that, in a criminal investigation, depending on the local legislation the questions that are taken as input to this process may be more or less important in setting the rules of what the forensic expert is allowed to do.

In the final process, *reporting*, the findings from the analysis are reported. The purpose of this step is mainly to report well-grounded answers to the questions given to the examiner in the previous step. In this step it is very common that new questions will arise in light of the provided answers, for that reason the last two steps are commonly iterative. It is also worth mentioning that it is of great importance that the conclusions drawn in this step are actually conclusions that are backed up by the findings during the examination. Each of the phases and considerations relating to each phase will be discussed in greater detail in Chaps. 4 and 5.

1.2 Questions and Tasks

Here are the questions for the first chapter, for these questions you may benefit from answering them in a group discussion!

1. Consider in what types of criminal investigations that computer forensic experts may be involved and in what way.
2. Consider when a computer forensic expert may be needed in a corporate environment.
3. Brainstorm on what types of devices that may be interesting to a computer forensic expert.
4. To whom are the findings of a computer forensic examination of interest?

References

Forensic control. (2017). Beginners guide to computer forensics. Available online https://forensiccontrol.com/resources/beginners-guide-computer-forensics/. Fetched July 6, 2017.

Reith, M., Carr, C., & Gunsch, G. (2002). An examination of digital forensic models. *International Journal of Digital Evidence, 1*(3), 1–12.

Chapter 2
What Is Cybercrime?

Abstract Computer forensic experts are commonly faced with the misconception that they work primarily on cybercrimes. The reality is quite opposite, namely that digital forensics is of importance in pretty much every possible type of crime ranging from computer intrusions to theft. This chapter provides a discussion on what cybercrime is, from the author's perspective. But more importantly, this chapter gives the reader a presentation on how and in what cases digital evidence can be of use during criminal investigations. The aim of the chapter is to make the reader understand that in the modern world, we leave digital traces almost all the time. We may not always be aware of this fact, but knowing and understanding how digital traces are left behind is of great importance for a computer forensic expert. For instance, even if a criminal is conducting a crime without so much as looking at her phone or computer, chances are that she is a using chat client to talk to some friend about what she did. This action can leave incriminating evidence that can be valuable in court.

Keywords Cybercrime · Digital evidence · Computer aided crime

Before dwelling deeper into forensics it seems reasonable to have a discussion on what signifies cybercrime. Or, maybe more importantly, how and when digital evidence comes in play during criminal investigations. I choose to include this discussion due to the fact that during my work as a forensic examiner, I was often faced with the misconception that my daily work was with cybercrime in the sense of computer hacking and that sort of things. In reality, digital evidence is present in crimes of almost every kind.

To begin this discussion, it is interesting to look at what Rogers wrote back in 2000. He uses the traditional approach of Means, Motive, and Opportunity to discuss cyber criminals. In this discussion Motive is the reason for why someone is committing a crime. Take defrauding for example, the common motive for defrauding someone is to earn money. Means would be the tools used to commit the crime and opportunity could be described as the possibility to commit the crime. One could argue that a crime begins in motive and that the means and opportunity

© The Author(s) 2017
J. Kävrestad, *Guide to Digital Forensics*, SpringerBriefs in Computer Science,
https://doi.org/10.1007/978-3-319-67450-6_2

are mere results of the easiest way to achieve what is wanted as motive. This way of thinking opens up the discussion on cybercrime to not only cover "hard" computer crimes such as hacking, but also to involve any crime that is aided by computers.

This view is further discussed by Rogers (2001), who described different types of computer criminals. On the topic of online fraudsters, he argued that online fraudsters are simply fraudsters that commit their crimes online. The same can be said about criminals that sell drugs online and that are involved in child exploitation crimes, and a wide range of other criminals. They are committing traditional crimes and have traditional motives, but they see the opportunity to commit the crimes from the comfort of their own house, using the Internet. Also, as of today, the means to commit the crimes becomes owning a computer and most people have a computer already.

In a study conducted by Kävrestad (2014), online frauds were examined to model and define the online fraud process. This study made it clear that there is no real difference between online and offline fraudsters, the difference lies in the way that the crime is committed. However, it should not go unnoticed that crimes committed online provide a criminal investigation with opportunities that are hard to come by in the case of crimes committed offline. This is due to the fact that actions carried out on a computer leaves traces and this fact gives a forensic examiner the chance to recreate and uncover what has happened. This data is often very valuable evidence.

As an end to this brief cybercrime discussion, we should not forget how digital evidence can play a big role even in crimes that are totally offline. Thing is, in modern society it is very hard to do anything without leaving digital traces. Even if you are doing something totally offline, in the heat of the moment or whatnot, there is a great chance that there can be digital evidence to support what happened. This can involve communication logs that can show what the criminal did after the crime was committed. Maybe he looked up punishments for the crime he committed, or even talked to some friend about what he did? I have even seen an example where a cell phone was used to tie a suspect to a crime scene, when the cell phone was not even used, it was just present!

2.1 Questions and Tasks

The task for this chapter is to get hold of two verdicts, then read them and consider how digital evidence what used in the cases. Try to get one verdict about a traditional cybercrime such as hacking or copyright infringement and one about something unrelated to the digital world, such as theft. In Sweden you can call a local court and have them send you verdicts over e-mail and you are often able to find verdicts online, just make sure you do not break any local laws!

References

Kävrestad, J. (2014). Defining, categorizing and defending against online fraud.

Rogers, L. (2000). Cybersleuthing: Means, Motive, and Opportunity. Available online:http://www. sei.cmu.edu/library/abstracts/news-at-sei/securitysum00.cfm [fetched 2017-05-01].

Rogers, M. K. (2001). *A social learning theory and moral disengagement analysis of criminal computer behavior: An exploratory study Doctoral dissertation*, University of Manitoba.

Chapter 3
Computer Theory

Abstract Perhaps the most important skill for someone working with computer forensics is to know how computers work. In order to locate digital traces of an e-mail, the examiner must know that such traces may look like. While this book is intended for someone who is fairly skilled in the computer world, there are some theories that are extra important for a forensic examiner and this computer theory is presented in this chapter. This includes an overview of encryption and decryption as well as a presentation of how data is represented in the digital word, in binary, hexadecimal and plain ASCII. Further, this chapter introduces theory that is often overlooked by disciplines other than computer forensics. This includes an overview of the NTFS file system and Windows registry that is one of the most valuable sources of information during an examination of a Windows computer. The chapter also describes what commonly happens when a file is deleted from a computer, namely that it is not deleted at all.

Keywords Windows registry · Encryption · Decryption · File structure · Data representation · Partitions

Up until this point, we discussed what computer forensics is and pretty much concluded that is it about examining and deducing what happened on a computer or in a computer system. That is all well and good, but to move on further you do need a bit of background knowledge. The intent of this book is not to provide you with a summary of computer science. Rather, I expect you to have a fair "know-how" on computer stuff. But there are a few areas that I found that IT people commonly do not know that much about, but that are important to a computer forensic expert. Those areas are covered, in brief, here. Note that each subsection is an overview. For a complete understanding—follow the references!

© The Author(s) 2017
J. Kävrestad, *Guide to Digital Forensics*, SpringerBriefs in Computer Science,
https://doi.org/10.1007/978-3-319-67450-6_3

3.1   Secondary Storage Media

Secondary storage media refers to media where data is stored for long-term preservation. This is in contrast to primary memory, which includes random access memory and cache memories, which is used for short-term storage. Secondary storage includes hard drives, CD/DVD, USB flash drives and memory cards. This discussion refers mainly to hard drives but is also (commonly) applicable for USB flash drives and memory cards.

The first thing that is important to know is the physical size of the storage media. This is because it is important to know that you can account for all the storage area on a computer. Say that you find a computer that appears to have a "C: \" partition of 200 GB, but a physical examination of the hard drive reveals that it is supposed to be able to house 250 GB of data. This could mean that there is another hidden partition present on the hard drive or that the hard drive was reformatted. Either way, the remaining 50 GB may contain valuable evidence.

This is also a good place to comment on how hard drive formatting is commonly handled by the operating system. It is easy to assume that if you repartition your hard drive, the existing data is overwritten. That is, most times, not the case. Rather, the hard drive is made up from sectors and clusters that can be allocated to a file or a partition. When you partition a hard drive you create a Master Boot Record or GUID partition table (other versions exist as well, but seems rare) that contains a partition table. The partition table houses information about partitions on the hard drive including starting and ending sector for each partition. If you resize your partitions the only thing that will happen is that the partition table gets updated. The actual data on the hard drive is often unaffected. While this makes the data that was on the hard drive inaccessible by the operating system it is still possible to recover it using forensic tools.

It should also be mentioned that it is quite common that a hard drive that may appear empty is just reformatted. When a hard drive is reformatted, it happens every so often that only the partitioning table is removed. The partitions, that we will discuss next, still remain on the disk. The reformatting only made it possible for the computer to put new data in the sectors that made up the partitions. But until that happens, the old data is still fully readable and the partitions can be recovered using forensic tools. Further information on hard drives and partition tables is beyond this book, but a good source of information is available at www.ntfs.com/ntfs (NTFS 2017).

3.2   The NTFS File Systems

As we just discussed hard drives and partitions, the next logical step becomes discussing file systems. A file system is essentially a structure used to control how data is stored and retrieved on a computer and is the common content of a partition.

So to make things clear: a hard drive contains partitions, a partition commonly contains a file system and a file system is used to structure data. I am saying that a partition *commonly* contains a file system because that is not always the case. For instance a partition may contain some semi-organized data such as swap space—but that is another story.

As for the file system, there are several different file systems out there such as ext4(common on Linux), NFS (common for network storage), and FAT32 (common on surveillance video and thumb drives). However, we will dig into the NTFS file system that is used on moderns Windows-based computers for the sole reason that NTFS is the most common encounter for a forensic examiner.

As previously discussed, the partitions are stated in the partition table found in the master boot record. Next, a partition formatted with the NTFS file system begins with a metadata file called the Partition Boot Sector. What we need to know about this file is that it contains the Master File Table (MFT) that is basically a dictionary of all files and folders on the NTFS partition. The most important content, for a forensic examiner, in the MFT is the file records. All files and folders on the partition have one! For each file or folder on the partition, the MFT record contains information about the name and the actual file data. However, a MFT record cannot be bigger than 1024 bytes; so files that are bigger than about 600 bytes (about 400 bytes is reserved for file name and such) cannot reside in the record. In these cases, the MFT record describes what clusters on the hard drive that house the file (Guidance Software 2016). Files contained in the MFT are called resident and files not contained in the MFT are called non-resident. Before we move on you should also know that there is a backup MFT, commonly located at the end of the partition (TechNet 2017).

So how are files created and deleted? Well, when you create a file or folder it will get a MFT record. If the file is small enough it will be stored in the MFT and if it is too big the computer will allocate clusters and store the file in the clusters. When you delete the file, it is actually the MFT record that gets deleted and the data in the allocated clusters remains there until they are overwritten. This allows a forensic examiner to recover deleted files using forensic tools. Do note that there is a technology known as trim that overwrites clusters that are unallocated by the MFT, this is quite commonly used for SSD hard drives.

3.3   File Structure

To be able to recover and understand files, you need to know a little bit about how files are commonly structured. You should know that a file does not need to follow a certain structure so what you read here is not always the case. Well then, the common structure of a file is that it begins with a header containing metadata and then comes the actual data and finally a trailer. The metadata commonly contains what is called a file signature that tells the computer what kind of file the file is, such as a JPEG or PDF. By knowing this you can search a hard drive for headers and

```
0000 | FF D8 FF E0 00 10 4A 46-49 46 00 01 01 01 00 78 | ÿØÿà · · JFIF · · · · · x
0010 | 00 78 00 00 FF DB 00 43-00 02 01 01 02 01 01 02 | · x · · ÿÛ ·C · · · · · · · ·
0020 | 02 02 02 02 02 02 02 03-05 03 03 03 03 03 06 04 | · · · · · · · · · · · · · · · ·
```

Fig. 3.1 Header of a JPEG file

```
000000 | 25 50 44 46 2D 31 2E 34-0D 25 E2 E3 CF D3 0D 0A | %PDF-1.4 ·âãÏÓ · ·
000016 | 34 20 30 20 6F 62 6A 0D-3C 3C 2F 4C 69 6E 65 61 | 4 0 obj ·<</Linea
000032 | 72 69 7A 65 64 20 31 2F-4C 20 35 30 31 35 32 37 | rized 1/L 501527
000048 | 2F 4F 20 36 2F 45 20 34-39 38 31 31 31 2F 4E 20 | /O 6/E 498111/N
000064 | 31 2F 54 20 35 30 31 33-32 38 2F 48 20 5B 20 34 | 1/T 501328/H [ 4
```

Fig. 3.2 Header of a PDF file

trailers to find files even if they are deleted from the MFT. You can do this by searching for the hexadecimal or alphanumeric file signatures depending on your software.

An example of a file signature is given in Fig. 3.1, which shows the file signature for a JPEG file. The left-hand side shows the file offset in hexadecimal (not relevant at the moment), the middle column shows the file data in hexadecimal and the right-hand side shows the file data in alphanumerical format. As you can see, the file begins with FF D8 FF E0 and this is what you would search for if you wanted to look for deleted JPEG files. You could also search for JFIF which is part of the alphanumerical file signature. Another example is given in Fig. 3.2, which shows a part of the header for a PDF file. In this case you would search for 25 50 44 46 2D or %PDF-1.4.

It is also worthwhile to mention that there are different approaches on how to store files. Most file formats, including plain text files and many picture formats, store files as plain files. However, some files including Microsoft office files are stored as compound files. Compound files are files that maintain some structured storage approach of their own (Microsoft 2017a). That means that there is a local file structure within the compound file. This is the common case for compressed files. What is special about compound files is that they cannot be fully examined when they are in their "packed" state. Instead, they must be unpacked to be fully analyzed. The reason is that the data in the compressed state is represented in a different way than in the original, unpacked state.

3.4   Data Representation

This section contains a very brief discussion on how data is stored and represented in a computer system. This is simply to make you understand that the data may have different meaning depending on how you interpret it.

Bits:	1	1	1	1	1	1	1	1	1
Value:	256	128	64	32	16	8	4	2	1

Fig. 3.3 Bits and values

To begin, the data stored on any storage media is stored in binary, with zeroes and ones. You may group the bits into groups of eight called bytes and a byte may also be represented with two hexadecimal signs. To make life complicated, different applications may store data in different order. To begin, when we are looking at a single byte, containing 8 bits, the order is always the same. You interpret the bits with the leftmost bit having the highest significance and the rightmost having the lowest, as depicted in Fig. 3.3.

That is all well, but when you have a dataset consisting of more than one byte we get in trouble. There are two ways to store consequent bytes. The first is called big-endian, storing bytes with the biggest end first making the first byte the most significant. In contrast we have little-endian storing data with the smallest end first, reading from left to right (Cohen 1980). To give an example—consider the word "troll" in little- and big-endian in Fig. 3.4.

That is that on binary and hexadecimal representation. You should just know that depending on what kind of data you are looking at you may want to look at it in binary or hexadecimal.

The final part on data representation is that you should know that computers have different ways of representing characters, called different ways of encoding data. While I have no intention of discussing different ways of encoding text or data you should know that different ways of encoding data exists, such as ASCII, UTF-8 and UTF-16. What the encoding decides is basically how a sign is represented in binary or hexadecimal code. For instance, the letter "A" is represented as "feff0041" in UTF-16 and as "41" in ASCII, using hexadecimal code. The reason why this is important is that if you open a dataset that is encoded in ASCII with a program that expects something else, the result will we screwed up.

Fig. 3.4 Example of little- and big-endian

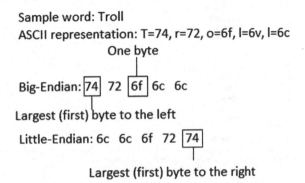

Sample word: Troll
ASCII representation: T=74, r=72, o=6f, l=6v, l=6c
One byte

Big-Endian: 74 72 6f 6c 6c
Largest (first) byte to the left
Little-Endian: 6c 6c 6f 72 74
Largest (first) byte to the right

3.5   Windows Registry

The Windows Registry is a hierarchical database that stores information about users, installed applications and the Windows system itself (Microsoft 2017b). That makes it a very important place for forensic examiners to look and something for this book to provide an overview of.

To begin, the Windows registry is a tree structure were each node in the tree is called a key, every key may have a value or sub-keys. A registry tree can be as deep as 512 keys (Microsoft 2017b). The values that a key can contain are just arbitrary data, it is up to the application that stored the value to decide the format and how it is to be interpreted. The registry is made up of several files, so-called hives (Guidance Software 2016). Each hive contains a set of data, the hives that are most commonly of interest to a forensic examiner are called SAM, SECURITY, SYSTEM, and SOFTWARE. There is also another file associated with each user called NTUSER.dat. There is one NTUSER.dat for each user on the system, this file is located in the user directory (…\Users\< username >). The other registry hives are located in the..\System32\config\ folder. You may extract the hives and analyze them with a forensic tool, such as AccessData Registry viewer. You may also examine the registry of a running Windows system through the built-in utility regedit. In Fig. 3.5, presenting an example of regedit, you can see that it presents the registry hives in a format that is a bit different than you may think. This is because regedit shows the registry as seen by the running computer.

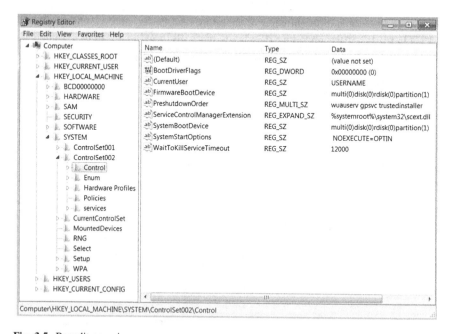

Fig. 3.5 Regedit overview

HKEY_CURRENT_USER contains the data stored in NTUSER.dat for the current user and data from the other hives is present in HKEY_LOCAL_MACHINE. In the picture you can see that there are several keys in the tree at the left and some values in the pane at the right. In this case, the values are located under the key "Control" that in turn is a sub-key to the key ControlSet002 that is in the SYSTEM hive.

As you may understand, the registry can be a huge database and many programs store data in the windows registry. I strongly suggest working with the registry to learn what kind of information that can be found in it. The rest of this section will cover each registry hive and the information found, in brief.

NTUSER.dat is a hive that stores information about a specific user account. This hive can for instance contain information such as the user's browser settings and history and data related to user applications.

SOFTWARE is the go-to hive for information related to applications. This includes data stored by Windows and data stored by other applications. A common piece of information to fetch here is the Windows version and install date, located in the sub-key \Microsoft\WindowsNT\CurrentVersion. This key will also tell you the registered owner of the computer and it is surprisingly common that a real name is set here. Note that dates are commonly NOT stored in human-readable format. For instance, the install date is stored as a UNIX timestamp—seconds that has passed since midnight on the first of January in 1970—this needs to be converted.

SYSTEM will contain information about the system including USB devices that has been connected to the system, time zone settings, and information about networks that the computer has been connected to. An example is given in Fig. 3.6 that shows you time zone information stored in the key \SYSTEM\ControlSet001 \Control\TimeZoneInformation\TimeZoneKeyName.

The *SAM* and *SECURITY* hives are protected by the Windows system and cannot be browsed using regedit on a running computer. However, extracting them from a forensic image and browsing them using a forensic tool is no problem. The *SAM* hive basically stores information about users. Examining this hive you can, for instance, find the users on the local machine, information about when they last logged on, when each account was created and password hashes. Finally we have

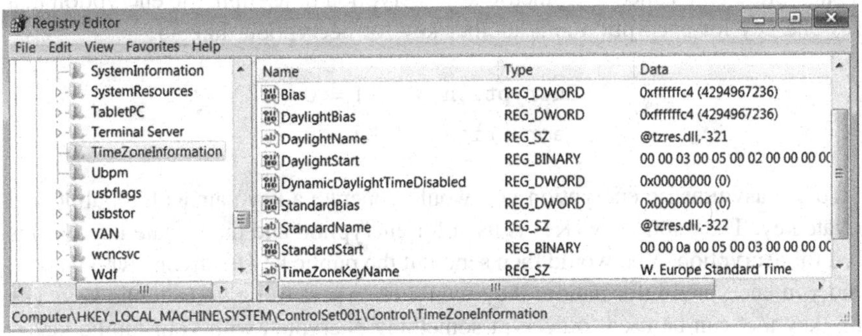

Fig. 3.6 Time zone information in the registry

the *SECURITY* hive that stores some information about the system, perhaps mainly the system audit policy and the Syskey that you will need in addition to the *SAM* hive if you need to crack user passwords.

3.6 Encryption and Hashing

There are tons of good books for you to read if you want to get down and dirty with encryption and hashing, but for the purpose of this book I will just discuss the terms very briefly. Encryption and hashing are cryptographic techniques used to hide data. Understanding how this works is crucial for a forensic expert because, well, criminals usually do not want their data to be analyzed. Also, in modern computers, encryption and hashing are usually built-in, fundamental parts of the normal computer behavior.

Beginning with encryption, encryption is the process of taking some dataset and a key, run it through an encryption algorithm and then you get a cipher text that is not readable. To get you up to speed on the terminology, the data you input is called (P)laintext, then we have the (K)ey and the resulting (C)ipher text. It is common to describe the encryption process as an equation, like so

$$P + K = C$$

The cipher text can be reverted to the plaintext by the process of decryption, in which you pass the algorithm the cipher text and the key, like so

$$C + K = P$$

The process just described is called symmetric key encryption or just symmetric encryption. This is because the same key is used for both the encryption and decryption. This introduces a problem when you want to share encrypted information with someone. In this case, you need to share the key beforehand because the receiving person will need the key for decryption. To meet this demand there is an encryption type called asymmetric key encryption or asymmetric encryption that uses one key for encryption and another key for decryption, like so

$$Encryption : P + K1 = C$$
$$Decryption : C + K2 = P$$

To use asymmetric encryption you would generate a key pair with a public and private key. The public key (K1) is used for encryption and the private key (K2) is used for decryption. You would then send out the public key to anyone who want to send you encrypted information; they would encrypt it using your public key. The only key that can be used to decrypt something encrypted with your public key is your private key, you keep that to yourself. Asymmetric encryption has several other usages, well beyond the scope of this book.

Hashing is a cryptographic technique that is used more for storage of sensitive data and validating data integrity than sharing encrypted information. A hash algorithm is basically a one-way function that takes a (P)lain text as input and produces a (H)ash value, or digest. What is important about a hash function is the property of it being one-way, meaning that it is impossible to derive the P from the H. The hash function can be described like so:

$$P \rightarrow H$$

For a hash algorithm to be considered secure it must have the following properties:

- Collision resistant meaning that there is only one H for each P
- Irreversible meaning that it is impossible to derive P from H.

The two main usages for hashes are storing some kinds of sensitive data, like passwords, and to fingerprint data in order to ensure data integrity. In terms of ensuring data integrity hashing is used as a fingerprint. If you want to send someone a message, you can create a hash value for the message and send the message and the hash to the recipient. The recipient can then hash the message and compare his hash value to the one you sent to him. Since the hash algorithm is collision resistant, matching hashes will ensure that the message was not altered. In terms of storing passwords they are commonly stored in a hashed format, this is the case in Windows operating systems. When a user wants to log in, she will submit her password to the system and the system will run what she enters through the hashing algorithm and compare that hash value to the one stored in the user database. If the hashes match the password must be correct and the user is allowed to enter the computer.

3.7 Decryption Attack and Password Cracking

As we have already discussed, it is quite common that the subject of a forensic examination uses encryption to hide data that can be valuable for the forensic examiner. For that reason it is vital that a forensic expert has some know-how on how to crack encrypted files and passwords. The methods for breaking encryption and hashing can roughly be divided into two different methods—Decryption attack and Password cracking. The rest of this section will describe them both.

A decryption attack is where you attack the encryption or hashing algorithm or implementation of it to deduce the plaintext from the cipher or digest. Using this kind of attack will save you the trouble of trying to guess the password, a time-consuming approach. However, the most common encryption and hashing algorithms do not suffer any known weaknesses that make this kind of decrypting attack feasible in a forensic examination. You should, however, know about the existence of this approach, because every so often you stumble upon some old and weak algorithm. Whenever you are about to attack some application or algorithm that you are not familiar with I encourage you to research it to determine the best point of attack.

Even if you are not able to attack the actual encryption algorithm, there may be weaknesses in how it was implemented. You may uncover such a weakness by experimenting on how a software works. This was actually the case for me and a colleague of mine a couple of years back. We worked a case were the suspects used a website called Privnote to send encrypted messages that destroyed themselves upon being read. We could find traces of the messages on the suspect's computer but they were encrypted. After examining Privnote we realized that when you sent someone a link to a Privnote message you had to give them a URL, and the URL contained the key used for encryption. We could also deduce that the AES algorithm, which is a symmetric encryption algorithm, was used for encryption. That told us that we should be able to harvest possible keys from the computers browsing history and then use whatever we found to decrypt the messages we uncovered, and we could.

The most common case is that a decryption attack is not possible. In that case you need to resort to password guessing. Technically, a password guessing attack against an encryption scheme means that you try different keys until you get a result. This works because a basic property of an encryption algorithm is that if you supply an algorithm with the wrong key, it will return nothing. That way you can know that if you get something, you get the Plaintext. You could express this in an equation, like so

$$\texttt{Unsuccessful attempt} : C + K_{wrong} = \texttt{Nothing}$$
$$\texttt{Successful attempt} : C + K_{correct} = P$$

Password guessing against hash algorithms works a little bit different, because there is commonly no key to submit. Instead you need to hash different data sets and compare that hash values that you get with the one you want to crack. When you get a hash value matching the value you want to crack you are done. Consider a case where you want to crack the digest $H_{tocrack}$ by hashing multiple different P, called P_{test}. For a successful attempt the H for P_{test} would be equal to $H_{tocrack}$, like so

$$P_{test} \rightarrow H_{tocrack}$$

Given that P_{test} is the wrong plaintext you would get some other value as H.

Now that you know the basics of password guessing it is time to get a bit practical. There are two ways to do a password guessing attack, brute force and dictionary. Using a brute-force attack you try every possible combination of signs until you get to the correct one. This attack can be quite feasible on short passwords but totally impossible to succeed with for longer passwords. Consider a situation where you are able to test 10 billion passwords in 24 h. This is a quite reasonable scenario. To calculate the total amount of possible passwords, the key space, you need to know the number of different signs and how many characters that are in the password. The formula you use to calculate the key space is taking the number of different signs to the power of *n* were *n* is the password length. Given that a password contains english upper and lower case letters and numbers you get 62 different possible characters. You can then calculate the average time to crack a password. You begin with calculating the time it takes to exhaust the key space. Dividing the key space with the number of attempts you can do in 24 h gives you how many days it takes to exhaust the key space. The rules of probability tells us that we will, on average, have to go through half the key space to find the correct password. Thus, the time it takes to crack a password can be expressed like so

$$(\mathtt{Key\ space/attempts\ per\ day})/2 = \mathtt{average\ cracking\ time\ in\ days}.$$

As an example, key space and cracking time for passwords of different length in our scenario is presented in Table 3.1.

As you can tell from the numbers in Table 3.1, cracking an eight character long password using a brute-force attack is very time consuming. Even if we give ourselves computer power enough to test 1000 billion passwords in 24 h it would still take us about 110 days to crack it. That is way too long, not to mention that passwords containing special characters or are even longer will take exponentially longer time to crack.

Fortunately, there is a more time-efficient method for password cracking, the dictionary attack. The dictionary attack is based on you creating a list of words and then testing so see if any of the words is the password. The computer resources needed for a dictionary attack are roughly the same as for a brute-force attack. The basics of a dictionary attack are simple—if the password is one of the words in your list—you will crack the password. If the password is not in the list it will not get cracked. Following that analogy, the successfulness of a dictionary attack is based on the attackers, yours, ability to make a good dictionary. Luckily, I can give you a method to work with!

To begin, we need to understand that computer users are often time quite predictable when they create passwords. It is very common for humans to use come kind of method for remembering passwords, and to use the same passwords for different services. This allows us to gather data and create a somewhat tailored wordlist for the person whose password we want to crack.

Table 3.1 Sample key space and cracking time for passwords

Password length	Equation	Resulting keyspace	Sample crack time in days
2	62^2	3844	0.0000002
4	62^4	14776336	0.00074
5	62^5	916132832	0.046
6	62^6	56800235584	2.85
7	62^7	3521614606208	176
8	62^8	218340105584896	10917

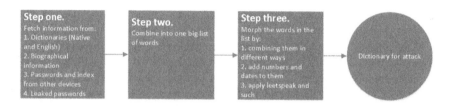

Fig. 3.7 Creating a dictionary for a dictionary attack

To begin creating a dictionary, I suggest that you start with a complete wordlist of all words in the English language and the language native to the person whose password you want to crack. Next step would be to gather information about the person such as interests, family, friends, and occupation. Then you find all possible worlds relating to that person and his interests—this is called biographic data—and input to your list. Then you would look into the data that you fetched from other devices owned by the person and look for passwords. If you find any, add those to your list. Getting close to the end its time to index devices owned by the person— this will generate a list of all words present on each device—then add those words to your list. As a final touch you should look online for leaked passwords from sites that this person may had an account on. Compiling all these pieces of information gives you a raw dictionary. To further enhance your chances of cracking the target password, you should now morph the words in the dictionary by combining them in different ways and by adding numbers and dates to them and so on. Following this process—visualized in Fig. 3.7—will give you a good chance to crack the target password.

Now I guess that you are saying that you will end up with a very large list and that is true. In my experience, the size of the list will be up to about two billion words. However, remember that with a reasonable amount of computer power you can test about ten billion passwords in 24 h making two billion attempts very reasonable.

3.8   Memory and Paging

Finishing up the part on computer theory I just want to mention some things about the memory and paging. The memory is an extremely valuable piece of information for the one reason that this is where the computer stores information relating to what it does at the moment. Also, the memory is emptied every time the computer restarts so the content in memory relates only to what the computer was up to since the last reboot. This makes information in the memory extremely good, because it is hard for a suspect that was arrested sitting in front of his computer to claim that someone else was responsible for the information found in the computer memory.

Further, when you are viewing encrypted data in a decrypted format the decrypted version of the data is temporarily stored is memory—this makes the memory a good place to find encrypted information in a decrypted state. During my personal forensic work I found passwords, encrypted e-mails and several pieces of incriminating evidence in memory.

Before leaving this topic, I want to mention that whenever the computer needs to hold more data in memory than the memory can hold, part of the memory is stored on the hard drive. This is a process called paging. On Windows systems, the "paged-out" parts of the memory are stored in the file called "pagefile.sys" and it can contain the same type of information as the memory. There are several methods on how to examine computer memory. Memory analysis will be covered in the practical section.

3.9 Questions and Tasks

Here are the questions for this chapter.

1. Brainstorm on what secondary storage media devices there are that can be of interest during a forensic investigation.
2. What happens when you delete a file from a NTFS file system and how can you recover deleted files?
3. What is meant with resident and non-resident files?
4. Why do you need to know the difference between little and big-endian?
5. Use regedit to find out what time zone your computer is set to use.
6. What is hashing and what signifies a secure hash algorithm?
7. What is the pro of a dictionary attack over a brute-force attack?
8. Why would you capture memory during a live investigation?

References

Cohen, D. (1980). *On holy wars and a plea for peace*. IETF. Available online https://www.ietf.org/rfc/ien/ien137.txt. Fetched July 6, 2017.
Guidance Software. (2016). *EnCase Computer Forensics II*. Guidance Software.
Microsoft. (2017a). Compound files. Available online https://msdn.microsoft.com/en-us/library/windows/desktop/aa378938(v=vs.85).aspx. Fetched July 6, 2017.
Microsoft. (2017b). Structure of the registry. Available online https://msdn.microsoft.com/en-us/library/windows/desktop/ms724946(v=vs.85).aspx. Fetched July 6, 2017.
NTFS. (2017). NTFS—New Technology File System designed for Windows 10, 8, 7, Vista, XP, 2008, 2003, 2000, NT. Available online http://www.ntfs.com/ntfs.htm. Fetched July 6, 2017.
TechNet. (2017). File systems. Available online https://technet.microsoft.com/en-us/library/cc938949.aspx. Fetched July 6, 2017.

Chapter 4
Collecting Evidence

Abstract Digital forensics is all about examining digital evidence and it implies that you need to collect the evidence before it can be examined. Every action that you carry out on a computer will leave traces and that contradicts with the facts that evidence must be handled in a way that ensures that it is not altered. This chapter discusses the key points of securing digital evidence in a forensically sound manner. Doing that ensures that the examination can be conducted in a way that does not contaminate the evidence. The concept of using a write blocker to create a forensic copy of the evidence is also introduced. The remainder of the chapter provides an in-depth discussion on live investigations, examining computers that are running. A model that can be used to plan forensically sound live investigations is presented as well as the constraints that must be taken into consideration when working with live evidence. ·

Keywords Disk image · Digital evidence · Live investigation

The first step in any forensic examination is to collect evidence. To begin, it is necessary to discuss what evidence, or more specifically, what digital evidence is. In general terms, evidence as a word means "The available body of facts or information indicating whether a belief or proposition is true or false" (Oxford Dictionaries 2017). This would of course state that digital evidence in turn would be the actual pieces of data that are used to draw conclusions. However, when you refer to a piece of digital evidence you commonly refer to a hard drive or cell phone or other carrier of digital information. For the sake of this book, digital evidence will mean "data collected from any type of digital storage that is subject to a computer forensic examination."

The key point in that definition is that everything that carries digital information can be subject to investigation, and any such carrier that is targeted for examination should be treated as evidence. This is due to the fact that in order to provide true results in a sound manner, all data that we examine has to be treated as evidence and there is, generally, no way of knowing what data in a data carrier that will be used to answer the questions in the examination.

© The Author(s) 2017

J. Kävrestad, *Guide to Digital Forensics*, SpringerBriefs in Computer Science,

https://doi.org/10.1007/978-3-319-67450-6_4

Well then, now that that is out of the way, the process of collecting evidence can in general terms be divided into one of two categories. The forensic examiner is either handed the devices subject for examination or is asked to take part in the actual collection. In law enforcement, this is comparable to the inspectors handing you the devices after they conducted a house search or actually asking you to participate in the house search. There is also a number of "in-betweens" where you may be handed devices that are on or you get to do a follow-up house search. However, from a forensic standpoint—what actually makes a difference in data collection is whether the device is powered on or off when the examination starts.

4.1   When the Device Is off

When the device is powered off, there is only so much you can do. There is only the data stored on the static memory, such as a hard drive, for you to examine. However, there is still some processing that needs to be done before you can analyze the actual data on the storage unit.

When conducting a forensic examination, especially in law enforcement, actions must be taken to eliminate any chance of modifying the actual evidence. You can see that starting a computer and browsing about is a big no-no. This is because every action that you take will, in some way, modify the original data and thereby contaminate the evidence. Contaminated evidence will in turn not be viable in court. For this reason, we need a way to make a copy of the evidence and then conduct out examination on the copy.

Under different circumstances, it is actually impossible or infeasible to not work on the actual evidence, different legislations will have different approaches on how to manage "live evidence"—the rule of thumb is to always document, in detail, what you do to live evidence.

As described by Lazaridis et al. (2016), it is of high importance that the copy is identical to the original data, in terms of content. To achieve such a copy, a so-called disk imaging software is used. The goal of any such software is to create a bit-by-bit copy of the original data and then conduct the examination on the copy. In forensic terms, the copy is generally called a disk image or a forensic disk image.

To create a disk image, the examiner needs to connect the data source that is subject to examination to a special device or an ordinary computer. She will then use a disk imaging software to create the actual disk image. Whenever you are connecting a storage unit to a computer it should be considered definite that something will be written to that unit. That does not comply with our forensic needs. To make sure that no alterations are made to the original evidence, write blockers are used when connecting a piece of digital evidence to a computer. As described by, for instance, Tobin et al. (2016), a write blocker is a device that is put between the digital evidence and the computer it is connected to and that prohibits the computer from writing any data to the device.

As a final step of creating a disk image, it is essential that you as a forensic expert can actually make sure that the copy is identical to the original. You may even need to testify to it! To make sure that the copy and the original is the same, hash comparison is used. The exact process varies between file formats but in essence, a hash of the original is created and then a hash of the copy is created. The hashes are then compared and if they match, the copy is identical to the original.

The concept of using disk imaging software and write blockers to create forensically sound copies of digital evidence is crucial in order to perform a forensically sound examination. The process and tools used vary in some sense depending on what type of device you are examining but the theoretical approach remains the same. A discussion on the tools used is not a part of this book.

4.2 When the Device Is on

In some cases, the device subject to examination is powered on when it comes into the hands of the forensic expert. This is commonly the case in a corporate environment or when the forensic expert is part of the team conducting a house search. When examining a computer or device that is turned on, a live examination, the examiner gets the opportunity to collect volatile data that includes information on what the device is currently up to. It also gives the examiner the opportunity to examine if any of the active hard drives are encrypted and collect unencrypted data from them. Common implementations of Full Disk Encryption (FDE) ensure that all data on the hard drive is encrypted when the computer is off. However, the data will be decrypted when the computer is on. Thus, before turning off a computer subject to examination, the examiner must make a thorough search for encryption tools. If any sign of encryption is present, the examiner should create a logical image of the hard drives to ensure that the data is preserved and available for later analysis.

The ultimate goal of a live investigation is to preserve as much volatile data as possible and ensure that data resting on hard drives is available for later analysis. Further, as a part of the house search, it is vital to ensure that you capture an overview of how the computer was set up, where it was located, and what peripheral devices were connected to it. Another important part of the house search is to look for any other devices that may be of interest to the investigation. As a part of this discussion, it must be stressed that good communication between the computer forensics expert, forensic experts from other disciplines and police officers on the case is of outmost importance. Above all else is that you secure the evidence that you need and that you, of course, comply with law and regulations.

Based on my own knowledge and experience, I created a process for a live investigation that describes the process in full, this is a good place to thank some of my previous colleagues for their review and criticism! A graphical overview of the process is presented in the picture in Fig. 4.1.

As the picture describes, you can abstract the process into three main steps; preparation, conducting, and afterthoughts. The idea is to visualize that to perform a

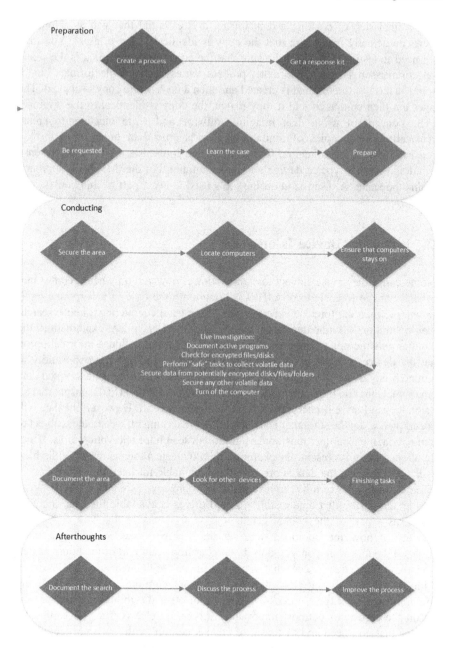

Fig. 4.1 Live investigation process

sound and good live investigation you need to prepare, and to learn from each investigation. The reminder of this chapter is devoted to careful explanation of each step in the process.

4.3 Live Investigation: Preparation

The preparation step is divided into two parts, one that is general (indicated by orange boxes) and one that should happen for every single house search. The general step is divided into creating a process and a response kit. The idea is that you should consider how you want to carry out live investigations in general. You can say that "Create a process" concerns putting words and deciding how to carry out the rest of the tasks in the process. Your process should cover a list of hardware and software you need, persons that are supposed to carry out live searches and preferably the competences needed. A personal tip, learned from carrying out quite a few live investigations is to also compile a list of numbers to persons that you may want to contact during the house search.

Next thing to do it is to assemble a response kit. A response kit is nothing more than a bag filled with the software and hardware you need to carry out live investigations. When you are putting together a response kit, you need to make sure that it can be used on any type of system you may encounter. Reading the rest of this book and/or learning about forensics in general will help you gather the knowledge you need to assemble your response kit! Apart from collecting USB thumbs, software's, write blockers and what not, you should remember that you may need supporting devices to make sure that you can get an internet connection, power or whatever you need to keep your tools going.

The blue boxes in the preparation step are concerned with the preparation related to the specific live investigation in question. It is not uncommon that you are requested to an ongoing house search and find yourself in a position where you have to "wing it". However, if you get the possibility you should carefully plan and prepare for you live investigation. The first planning step is to be requested, hopefully your organization got routines that makes sure that you are involved at an early stage in an investigation. If not, try to make them put such routines in place!

When you are requested, you have a chance to learn about what you are supposed to expect. Depending on the case and the settings of the house search, you can expect vastly different things. For instance, if you are working in legislation and supposed to do a live investigation of a system belonging to a computer technician suspected of child exploitation, there is a good chance that his system is encrypted. However, if you are working as a private investigator sent to examine the computer of an economic assistant suspected of stealing company client registers, you may want to look for information about USB devices.

When you learned about the case, you should make any preparations needed for the specific live investigation. This may include gathering additional tools and knowledge and can also include getting in contact with any other persons that are involved in the house search. In a police environment, it is common that police officers and other forensics experts are working the site at the same time. It is of outmost important that the group prepares together so that everyone knows who does what. You should also know what to expect from a security standpoint and how the police intends to enter and secure the building.

4.4   Live Investigation: Conducting

The conducting step involves all tasks that are performed "on-site". In this step, it is important to mention two things. First, depending on if you are working in legislation or in a corporate environment, you will have different rules and regulations that restrict how you may work. In a corporate environment, you are first and foremost restricted by the regulations local to the company. In legislation, you are restricted by law, and the law is different in different countries. For instance, in the US, it is common for a house search to target a specific device or piece of evidence and a lot of emphasis is put into preserving the chain of evidence. It is also of high importance that the evidence is handled according to the court decision and by authorized personnel. In Swedish legislation, a decision about a house search is often taken by a prosecutor and regards an entire home or area. It is also common that data stored on a cloud service or other remote location may not be subject to the house search decision. The ground rule is that you must have a good understanding of the rules and regulations that apply to you, and that you confirm that you are authorized to do what you plan with the head of the investigation.

Second, depending on the type of investigation and when you are called to the scene, all steps may not apply. Remember from the discussion about the preparation step—following each step in this model is a best case scenario. It is not always possible to follow the entire model.

So, before going on to describing each process in this step, I want to mention that you should take care to document everything you do. This is of outmost importance and it is very possible that you will have to account for your actions in court. Say that the suspect states that a computer you determined to part of a drug scam was never even connected to the Internet. If you documented how it was connected to a router with text and photo and made a connection test that you also documented, the suspects statement will never hold. However, if you failed to document, the court may find reason to question your findings. We will continue the discussion on documentation in the upcoming chapter.

Well then, before starting any house search, the entire team will travel to the site and enter the building in question. The first tasks at hand are to secure the building, locate any computers that are running, and ensure that they stay on. Depending on the case and background information, this can be done in a variety of ways. In an investigation of a severe crime were the suspects is likely to possess computer skills it is not uncommon to break in violently in order to surprise the suspect so that he or she does not turn off any computers as an attempt to hide evidence. In another situation you may simply knock on the door.

Securing the area is above all else in this step and it is the duty of the police officers. While the police officers secure the area, it is convenient if they look for computers that are turned on and make sure that they stay on. The computer forensic examiner can then enter the building after it is secured and start working on any computers that are turned on.

At this point, you could discuss if you should conduct the live investigations or document the area first. From my experience, you should never wait with the live investigation and this is for the sole reason that there are many ways to remotely erase data or there could be some software running that removes data upon certain events. Also, the task of documenting the area could be handed to a police officer.

Next is the main process in the house search, the live investigation. The live investigation should have the following ultimate goals:

- Document what is visually present on screen
- Collect volatile data
- Check if any data is encrypted and secure data from encrypted storage
- Provide clues for the continued house search.

Documenting what is actually present on screen is very important as it can prove to be very valuable evidence. This is primarily because of the fact that the stuff up on the screen was, evidently, visible to the person that was last sitting in front of the computer. The high value of this evidence is due to the fact that when you present a suspect with evidence from a hard drive, they commonly claim that they had no idea that they had that particular data on their computer. They may even state that it must have been put there by someone else or that they must have been hacked. However, if you are suspecting a person of selling drugs and you capture him sitting in front of a computer that is in fact being used to sell drugs at the very time that he is sitting there, those claims become harder to make. This corresponds to the first step in the live investigation process, Document active programs. This task involves taking photos of all active windows, documenting date and time settings and extracting other data from active processes, such as log files. This task would also, at least, include mapping of active network connections, document currently logged on users and testing the Internet connection. You may also want to check for connections to remote storage and recently plugged in USB devices.

> TIP: To ensure that data that you want to collect from the operating system you should create a script for this purpose. In appendix B, you can find scripts to do this collection on Windows, MAC and Linux—feel free to modify to suit your needs!

The next part of the live examination involves checking for evidence of encrypted data. This task would involve checking active processes to see if any process related to encryption is running and visually looking for encryption software. On Windows systems, you can see if a partition is encrypted with BitLocker by visually looking for a padlock on the partition icon in the computer menu. There is also a variety of tools to use to automatically detect encryption software and encrypted partitions. As a final task you can use imaging software to manually examine raw data for headers associated with encrypted volumes.

If you find that the computer contains encrypted partitions or encrypted data that is currently in a decrypted state you must secure this data to a logical disk image. However, the process of making a disk image during a live investigation is time consuming and you should consider capturing volatile date first. Volatile data is all data that will be lost when the computer is turned off, or data that is often changed. Thus, there is a good chance that the volatile data is modified by the disk imaging process. Collecting volatile data involves, at least, taking a snapshot of the computer memory (RAM) and gathering registry files. You should know that there are different ways to gather volatile data and some ways may risk that the computer crashes. For this reason, it is important to consider your actions. Volatile data, especially the memory, contains information that can help decipher what the computer has been up to since the last reboot. This is valuable information for the same reasons as for the active processes. Also, memory is commonly a good source for finding passwords and data from encrypted communication services in plain text. However, if the computer you are examining contains encrypted volumes and crashes during the memory capture, any potential evidence on the encrypted partition may be lost.

In my own experience, there are tools for memory capture that you can safely use without the computer crashing. One such tool, that is free to use is FTK imager that will be discussed in greater detail later. My recommendation is to capture any volatile data that you can using these "safe tools" and then create a disk image of possibly encrypted partitions and hard drives. Then you can move on to capturing volatile data in more "unsecure" ways if you need.

When you are done with all the steps you should make sure that you have documented everything that you have done and you can turn of the computer and bring it with you for further examination. Also note that in addition to looking for evidence relating the case you should also check if any remote storage is connected to the computer and if any USB devices have been connected to it. This information will assist you in your continued house search. Please also note that depending on the type of investigation, you may want to conduct live investigations on networking equipment as well as computers.

When any live investigations of running computers are done, you should make sure that the area is well documented. This would usually involve taking photos. This is important in order to know where stuff was. In the next process, it is time to search the rest of the area for any other interesting finds. In your role as a computer forensic expert, you will commonly look for any other device that can possibly be used to store information. This involves CD/DVD, USB drives, hard drives, and more. You should also make sure that you look for physical documentation that could be of interest, this could involve passwords, URL's, and other information that have been written down.

As finishing tasks, you should make sure that everything is documented and that all seized evidence is marked according to the regulations and routines that apply to you.

4.5 Live Investigation: Afterthoughts

When the house search is done, there are some finishing touches to attend to. First thing to do is to write a protocol that describes what was done and any possible findings during the live investigating. The responsibility of documenting may vary between different legislations but at the very least, you should document what you have done during the live investigations. A longer discussion on documentation will be held in the upcoming chapter.

After documenting, the team conducting the house search should discuss how the house search was performed. Ideally, this process would be conducted with police officers and any other forensic experts. But at the very least, you should consider the house search from a computer forensic perspective and update your own process as needed.

4.6 Questions and Tasks

Here are the questions for this chapter.

1. Why do you want to capture memory during a live investigation?
2. What is a forensic disk image?
3. What is volatile data?
4. Elaborate on the benefits of preparing before a live investigation and give examples on how to prepare.
5. Why would you prefer to analyze a forensic disk image rather than a live computer?

References

Lazaridis, I., Arampatzis, T., & Pouros, S. (2016). Evaluation of digital forensics tools on data recovery and analysis. In *The Third International Conference on Computer Science, Computer Engineering, and Social Media (CSCESM2016)*.

Oxford Dictionaries. (2017). Definition of evidence in English. Available online https://en.oxforddictionaries.com/definition/evidence. Fetched July 6, 2017.

Tobin, P., Le-Khac, N. A., & Kechadi, M. T. (2016). A lightweight software write-blocker for virtual machine forensics. In *Sixth International Conference on Innovative Computing Technology (INTECH) 2016* (pp. 730–735).1 IEEE.

Chapter 5
Analyzing Data and Writing Reports

Abstract This chapter describes the actual examination process and the general demands for a forensic examination. A basic rule is that the results presented in a forensic examination must be objective and true. Digital forensics is comparable to academic work in this manner. This chapter discusses the key concepts used to ensure that the results of a forensic examination meet those demands and discusses the concepts of being unbiased and producing reproducible results. The final target of any examination is to provide answers to some question or request. This chapter ends with a discussion on reporting and includes a scale that can be used to grade the strength of the conclusions drawn during the examination. As it is of great importance that a forensic report is interpreted the same way no matter who the reader is, using a common scale is of great help. Further, this chapter aims to provide the reader with an understanding of the key elements in the forensic process.

Keywords Examination · Reporting · Forensic analysis

For the final part of the theoretical section, we will discuss how to analyze data and write reports. This is the step where you work with the evidence that you collected in a sound manner in the previous step. That would for instance include forensic disk images and memory dumps. In general, you would always complete your analysis on these copies. However, in some cases, it is not possible to get a forensic image and in these cases, you would have to analyze the actual device directly. Different regulations for how to manage these cases exist in different legislations. At the very least, make sure you document WHY you had to investigate the device directly and what you did!

Okay then, analyzing data and writing reports are processes that are tied very closely together, the analysis is what you do and the report should describe your analysis and conclusions. While that sounds quite easy the reality is a bit more daunting. First, there are rules and regulations that decide what you can do and how you should do it. Then you need to consider that the audience of your report is usually not very good with computers but they still need to understand. To begin

© The Author(s) 2017
J. Kävrestad, *Guide to Digital Forensics*, SpringerBriefs in Computer Science,
https://doi.org/10.1007/978-3-319-67450-6_5

this discussion, I want to say that the rest of the chapter is written from a law enforcement perspective. This is because you are commonly more restricted when working with criminal investigations than when working with corporate investigations. Within a corporate environment, you can basically do whatever your manager tells you to (with reason of course….).

5.1 Setting the Stage

Before we move on, there are some general guidelines that should be followed when conducting a forensic examination. These guidelines are of different importance in different legislation, but for me they must always be followed in order to ensure a sound and fair investigation. A general rule in criminal investigations is that everyone is innocent until proven guilty and that investigations should not aim to prosecute a specific person but to uncover the truth. In the bigger picture, this is achieved in different ways including that suspects have the right to a proper defense, investigations should be unconditional and transparent and the defense should be able to know how conclusions were reached so that they can be disputed.

In many ways, this is similar to the foundations of scientific research where it is dictated that any study should be done in an unbiased and transparent way that allows for reproduction of the study. There are even more similarities in that a forensic investigation, much like a research project, aims to provide an answer to a question, i.e., are there any evidence of this computer being involved in an online fraud scheme?

So before we move on, we should just highlight that during the analysis and report writing, the forensic expert has to make sure that his work meets the following requirements:

Unbiased meaning that incriminating and exonerating evidence are considered and taken into account. In reality, this would mean that if you are asked to see if a computer was used during a specific period of time, you should put an equal amount of effort into evidence supporting the opposite, namely that it was not used. The bottom line is that it should not be important for the forensic examiner to find incrimination evidence, rather it should be important to find a correct and objective answer.

Reproducible meaning that you document the basis for you conclusions well enough for someone else to replicate your analysis. The general idea is that if someone does the same thing you have done they will reach the same conclusion. A big part of this property is also to provide transparency meaning that you account for all your findings as well as the methods you used. This has to, of course, be applied with sense. For instance, if the aim of your analysis is to find pictures you may not need to account for e-mail history on the investigated device. Also, if you are asked to get a list of the files on the computer desktop you do not need to document that you browed your way to the desktop and wrote down the file names. However, if you were asked to see if a computer was remote controlled and conclude that found no such evidence, you should document how you searched for remote control software, how you analyzed firewall logs, and so on.

As a final point to discuss, I want to stress the importance of using some clear and preferably standardized way of expressing conclusions. For instance, you may do an analysis with the aim of investigating if some pictures were taken in a specific place. Depending on what information you find, it is important to express your conclusion in a way that gives a just presentation of the evidence. Consider a case where you manually could see that the wallpapers in the said pictures matched the place that you were asked to match the picture against. This would be an indication that the picture was from that location, but it would not be a decisive piece of information. If you could also find GPS coordinates, matching the location, embedded in the picture you could go further and say that your investigation strongly suggests of even shows that the picture was taken in the suggested location. That being said I would suggest using a seven graded scale that is heavily influenced by the one that is being used by the Swedish police. The steps of the scale and how to express them are presented in Table 5.1.

Being able to express yourself in a way that gives a just view of your analysis and that provides enough punch to the investigation can be really hard and takes practice. But when you are making your conclusions you should try to argue with yourself and also have a colleague challenge your conclusions to make sure that they hold!

Table 5.1 Scale of expressions for conclusions

Expression	Explanation
The analysis shows that .... did not...	The key point here is first "shows that", this is a completely decisive expression and combined with a negation, did not, it can be used to claim that something did not happen. This expression should be used with care since it is often hard to claim that something did not happen with absolute certainty
The analysis strongly suggests that .... did not ...	Same as above but leaving room for an alternative explanation for the found evidence. However, when saying that your analysis strongly suggest something you are saying that you do not see any other plausible explanation for the evidence found
The analysis indicates that .... did not	"Indicates that" basically says that what you are saying is likely but it is quite possible that some other explanation is also true
The analysis is inconclusive	Inconclusive is to be used when your analysis does not really provide evidence that says anything about what you supposed to look for, or when the evidence is saying different things
The analysis indicates that	In this case, you analysis indicated that some statement was true, however other possibilities are plausible
The analysis strongly suggests that	Your analysis shows that something is true, other explanations are possible but not plausible
The analysis shows that	Your analysis shows that something is true

5.2 Forensic Analysis

Well then, having discussed the boundaries and requirements on a forensic analysis, it is time to get at it. First off, remember from the discussion in Chap. 1. That a forensic analysis is basically about answering question that the investigation has. To answer the question, you must analyze the data found on the forensic images you created in the "Collect evidence" phase. You may also have some other data that you collected during a live investigation. As a final point, you should also be aware that it is common to include information from other sources, such as interrogations or whatever seems reasonable in your case.

Giving some attention to questions that you may be asked by the investigators you should know that it can be about almost anything. It is often the case that the investigators do not really know that to ask for and your expertise in forensics is usually needed to clarify the purpose of the forensic investigation. Further, it should also be noted that when you report your findings in relation to one question, it is common that the investigators have follow-up questions that results in a new analysis. Also, the nature of the questions may range from "Is this picture resent in the suspect's computers" to "Find all incriminating or exonerating evidence in relation to online fraud". Your task as a forensic examiner is to find the underlying questions and bring conclusions for those.

Another thing worth mentioning is whether or not to stray from the purpose of the analysis and look for "other" information. In my opinion, there are two ways you should handle this dilemma. First of all, I think that there are some basic information that you should always uncover from every computer that you investigate. What information that should be included in this basic set of information would differ from legislation to legislation as well as between departments. But one thing you should know is that you must be prepared to take the stand and be a witness under oath, in court. And in my own experience, there are some questions that are very common to get and that you would like to have answers to, thus starting every analysis with gathering some common information is recommended! The second part of "other" information would be information that may be related to crimes but not directly to the question you are set to answer. The way you should treat this kind of information is strongly depending on your legislation and on occasions, the conditions in the search warrant. I would strongly suggest that you make notes about this type of information and discuss it with the lead investigator or prosecutor!

The discussion that we just had leads us to the process of a forensic analysis. One could just say that you should take your questions and find data that helps in answering them, but I would suggest using a more structured approach. Using a structured approach makes it easier to ensure that all evidence is treated in the same way and that all investigations are handled in a similar fashion no matter who the examiner is. In Fig. 5.1, I have tried to give a quick overview of how a forensic

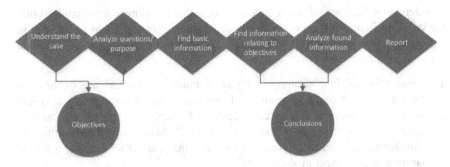

Fig. 5.1 Overview of a forensic process

process could be structured. The first step would be to get an understanding of the case at hand. Getting an understanding of the case you are working with will help you get a better idea of what to look for. This step would normally include reading about how the investigation got started, what types of evidence that are present in the case and transcripts from interrogations with suspects and witnesses in the case. All of this information is information that will help you understand the person that was supposedly using the computer you are examining and could include important information for your analysis such as the suspects explanation for different pieces of evidence, other persons involved in the case and how the supposed crimes were committed.

The second thing that you should analyze is the questions from the investigator. This makes out the actual purpose for your analysis. What you must know here is that the investigators are not always too good at asking questions or specifying a purpose, it is even common that the devices to analyze are just handed to the forensic examiner with no question or purpose at all. In these cases, I would encourage asking the investigators what they expect you to do, what outcomes are they hoping for and expecting. On the other hand, you must expect that questions will be very narrow or broad depending on the investigation. In this sense, "Find out all you can about this device in relation to this narcotic case" is a purpose that is just as legitimate as the question "Was this picture taken at the suspect's home address?" What the forensic examiner should do in this step is to use what she knows about the case and analyze the questions/purpose of the investigation to establish her own objectives with the investigation. This is where you use your expertise to decide what you should look for and how. Also note that depending on what you find during your analysis, you may need to add additional objectives.

When you established what to actually look for you should go into the process of actually looking for evidence. The first thing I encourage you to do is to find some basic information. This would be a step that you carry out for each and every one of the computers that you examine. The information you find during this step will make sure that you do not miss something fundamental and will, in my own experience, be very useful when appearing in court. Deciding what should go into the set of basic information is up to you or your manager and could be decided in legislation. However, the following list is a suggestion from me on what should, at least, be included.

1. *Account for all data* meaning that you examine the physical size of the hard drive and then look at how much of this space that is allocated to a visible partition. If a drive is able to carry 250 GB but only 200 GB are allocated to active partitions, the other 50 GB may contain a hidden or encrypted partition or something else. You will have to figure out if the data not allocated to a visible partition is of interest to your analysis.
2. *Get computer install date, operating system version, list of users, and registered owner* so that you can easily answer questions about what operating system the computer used, how many users there was on the system and so on.
3. *Get time zone information and clock settings* for the sole reason that times are commonly an important factor.
4. *Find network drive maps* so that you can know if the computer has been connected to remote storage media.

Next, you should get working on the objectives that you previously established. What you are going to do here is heavily dependent on what your objectives are. Your ability to complete these steps is of course what makes you a forensic expert and some common objectives and tasks will be explored in the practical section of this book. However, there is one aspect that needs attention. You will surely do most of you investigative work using well proven forensic tools. However, there may be times when you have a need to use tools you never heard about or tools that you even made yourself. To ensure that your investigation is fully transparent, it is of great importance that you document these tools. On the same topic I want to stress, once again, that the work you do in this step should be done in an objective way. You are supposed to look for evidence that is in favor as well as in opposition to your objectives. Your aim is not to make someone committed of a crime but to provide a just view of what happened.

When you completed your investigation and used different methods to search through the data on the computer you are examining it is time to analyze the information you found and draw conclusions. What is notable about this step is that your conclusions are reflecting the way that you interpret the data. Also, as previously discussed, it is important that you draw conclusions in a way that ensures that your conclusions are strong enough, meaning that you should not be afraid to actually make the statements that are backed up by your evidence. However, you must also make sure that you "do not claim too much" meaning that, well, your conclusions must actually be supported by your findings. A neat way to find the right balance is to debate your conclusions in a critical manner with yourself as well as with your colleagues.

When you have done your analysis, it is time for the final task of reporting your findings in a good report, and that deserves a section of its own.

5.3   Reporting

The final step in a forensic analysis is to write a report. The report basically serves two purposes. First it is where you present your *objective* findings and then you may include your conclusions based on the findings. As such, it is important to understand that the conclusions will always depend on your knowledge and interpretation of your findings, thus the conclusion is in some sense subjective. The content of a report will differ depending on legislation and local policies. However, it is common that all reports include;

1. Case data
2. Purpose of examination
3. Findings
4. Conclusions.

The reminder of this section will describe common information and considerations found in each part of the report. A sample template report is presented in Chap. 15.

5.3.1   Case Data

Case data, or similar in a criminal setting is simply information that describes the investigation that the examination is part of. Case data would include the name of the person that ordered the examination, some identifier of the investigating it concerns and information that identifies the evidence pieces that are subject to examination. Key point here is to maintain chain of custody or similar as well as being able to distinguish the examination from other examinations. The exact information that should be contained in the report is heavily dependent on local regulations and legislation.

5.3.2   Purpose of Examination

The purpose of the examination should be expressed in the report for the reason that it presents what you have been looking for during your examination. It is unreasonable to assume that an examination of one or more computers can produce a complete overview of all data on all storage devices. Therefore, expressing the purpose of the examination describes the focus of the examination and gives the reader an understanding of what he can expect as results.

Stating the purpose begins with the question or purpose that was expressed by the one who ordered the examination. It could, however, also include any objectives that the forensic examiner identified when analyzing the case. One example of a purpose statement could be as follows;

> The purpose of this examination was to identify if documents stolen during the break-in at samplestreet 41 was present on the computer. The suspect stated, in an interrogation, that the computer was hacked. Thus, the examination also included looking for evidence of remote control software, malicious software and evidence of intrusions

It should be mentioned that the nature of the purpose statement is very versatile depending on the needs of the investigation, the nature of the examination or the local procedures. In some cases, the forensic expert may only be tasked with gathering data from the device for someone else to analyze, in that case the problem statement could be;

> The aim of the examination was to extract all pictures from the device

In contrast, in some cases the examination that is conducted by the forensic expert is much more comprehensive. However, if the purpose of an examination becomes too widespread, it is sound to consider splitting the examination into several smaller examinations. To achieve that you could conduct one examination, or at least produce one report, for each step in the examination. For instance, it is common for examinations of computers suspected to be involved in online fraud scams to include looking for and analyzing pictures, recovering e-mails, recovering chat logs, analyzing browsing history, and more. Creating one report for each of those purposes would likely make the conclusions more understandable and increase the readability of the reports. In reality, it is advisable to discuss the way that the reports are created with the recipient of the report(s).

5.3.3 Findings

Presenting findings include presenting the pieces of evidence that you found during your examination. Findings should be presented in an *objective* manner meaning that you should present the pieces of information that you found, as is, and not make any subjective conclusion or interpretation. In essence, you could say that you should present and describe exactly what the information you present is telling you. For instance, consider a case where the forensic examiner was asked to analyze if some pictures were taken at a suspect's apartment. To fulfill this purpose, the examiner would look for GPS coordinates in the picture metadata. As findings, the forensic examiner will present the GPS coordinates and possible state if they match the coordinates of the suspect home address or not—these are objective facts. However, stating that the picture is actually from the suspect's apartment would be a subjective conclusion that needs more information.

5.3.4 Conclusions

The last piece of information that is commonly present in a forensic report is conclusions drawn by the forensic expert. What differs conclusions from findings is that a conclusion made by the forensic expert is based on the findings, her knowledge, and experience. That makes the conclusion *subjective* and a very important aspect of writing a forensic report is to clearly separate objective findings from subjective conclusions. A common way to indicate the strength of the conclusions is to use a scale that is common in the organization or jurisdiction. An example of such a scale was presented in Table 5.1 earlier in this chapter. An interesting point to discuss is that the notion of including conclusions in a forensic report is something that not everyone agrees on. Some professionals think that subjective information in a forensic report is just plain wrong. However, one cannot neglect the fact that the computer forensic expert is the person that is best suited to draw conclusions from the findings of her examination. What remains certain is that conclusions must be clearly stated and separated from the *objective* findings.

5.4 Final Remarks

As a final note on the process of performing and reporting on a computer forensic analysis, it is important to mention that no examination is the same as the other. This is demonstrated by the broad range of different devices that may be subjects to a forensic examination and the broad range of questions that may be asked by the investigation. While this makes it unpractical, if not impossible to follow a common process in every single examination, the ground rules are still the same. The most important knowledge is to understand that forensic examinations must be conducted and reported in a way that is unbiased and reproducible. This ensures transparent processes that can hold for scrutiny.

Further, claiming that there is one single tool or method that should always be followed is equally hard as determining one common process. While working as a computer forensic examiner, it becomes evident that different tools have different strengths (and weaknesses). It also becomes evident that there are cases when the most common tools are not able to do what is needed as the moment. In these cases, it is tempting to develop your on tools or use tools that are less common and that may be a feasible way to go. However, it is of outmost importance that a forensic examiner understands that the need for detailed documentation increases when you stray from the common path. All to ensure that the transparency of the examination.

Something that has been touched but not fully discussed in this book is what you have the right to examine. This discussion is much up to local laws and regulations but it should not go unnoticed that you need to know what you seized and what your warrant covers. It is very common to find references to data stored in the cloud. Cloud data would include a long list of services including online storage such as Google drive and e-mailing services. It is a very common practice that data that is stored online is off-limits. This is due to the fact that a warrant will cover an actual computer or physical location. Thus, if you seize a computer, you get access to the data stored on that computer. A general recommendation it to never follow references that are taking you online, at least not without asking a prosecutor. However, it is often possible to find traces of cloud data that is lingering in temporary files, slack space, memory or likewise. That information is, at least in Sweden, up for grabs.

As a final note on the theoretical section it must be stressed, once again, that while this book presents strategies that describe considerations and processes common to computer forensic examinations, the local laws, and regulations often dictate requirements that a computer forensic examiner must follow. Thus, what you read in the theoretical section is an overview of practices that you should consider. However, the actual implementation of the forensic processes is dictated by local regulations!

5.5 Questions and Tasks

Here are the questions for this chapter.

1. The results presented during a forensic examination should be unbiased and reproducible. What does this mean and why is it important?
2. In Fig. 5.1, an overview of a forensic process was presented. Describe all steps in brief.
3. Why is it important to report conclusions using a standardized scale?
4. Consider a case where you found references to files located at a Dropbox account. You then found the credentials to said account. Is it ok for you to download the files stored in Dropbox.

Part II
Put it to Practice

Now that you have some theoretical background. I am sure that you are eager to dig into more practical matters. In this part, you will find a practical discussion on how some common computer forensic tasks are done. The part begins with a chapter dedicated to methods for collecting data, it then continues with a chapter on finding artifacts that forensic experts are commonly set to find, and ends with a discussion on how to answer some very common questions that forensic experts are commonly challenged with. Before we begin, you should know that the objectives of an examination differ from case to case and that there are many more tasks that could be performed than those I present. Also, you do not need to go through everything every time.

Also, to do a forensic examination you will need a toolbox. As discussed earlier, I have used the Forensic Toolkit from AccessData for the purpose of this book, but there are many more open- source and proprietary tools out there to discover, each with their own strengths and weaknesses. For reference, an overview of the AccessData products used in this book is given in Chap. 10.

Chapter 6
Collecting Data

Abstract The common and best practice during a forensic examination is to create a bit-by-bit copy of the storage device that you are set to examine and then analyze the copy. Working in this manner ensures that the actual storage device is not contaminated and can even provide performance benefits. This chapter begins with a description of how to create this bit-by-bit copy, called disk image, using the tool FTK imager. The chapter then describes how to collect volatile data including taking a memory dump and extracting registry hives from a Windows computer. At times, you find a computer that is turned on and you are not able to extract any data from the computer because it is logged out or likewise. In those cases, it is possible to extract information from memory using invasive techniques. This chapter introduces two such techniques, DMA attack and cold boot attack. At the end of the chapter, some constraints and considerations relating to collecting video from surveillance equipment are presented.

Keywords Disk image · Imaging · Memory dump · Cold boot attack · DMA attack

A forensic examination will most likely begin with collecting data. As previously discussed you may want to collect data from different sources such as hard drives, windows registry, and volatile sources. Collecting data from different sources is discussed in this chapter. As a final treat, I included a short discussion on collecting data from video surveillance systems, as this can be a tedious task that often falls into the hands of a forensic examiner.

6.1 Imaging

Imaging is the process of copying a hard drive or other secondary storage media into a forensic image that can be used for the forensic examination. An important aspect of a forensic examination is to ensure that the actual data on the hard drive

© The Author(s) 2017
J. Kävrestad, *Guide to Digital Forensics*, SpringerBriefs in Computer Science,
https://doi.org/10.1007/978-3-319-67450-6_6

that is to be examined is not compromised and the only way to fully do that is by making a forensic image and then examine the image. Working with an image instead of examining the actual hard drive also brings other benefits, it usually enhances performance.

The best and safest way to create a forensic image is by making a physical image of a hard drive. To do this, you physically remove the hard drive from the computer and connect it to your own computer using a write blocker. A write blocker is a device that prohibits your computer from writing to the hard drive. If you are not using a write blocker, it is almost certain that your computer will write some data to the hard drive you are to examine, thus compromising the evidence. When you connected the hard drive to your computer, you can use your imaging software to create a physical disk image. Note that a physical disk image will create a copy of the hard drive from the first bit to the last giving you an identical copy of the hard drive that you are to examine. Also note that even if you have to image a running computer you may still do a physical image as long as the hard drive is not encrypted.

If the hard drive is encrypted, a physical image will do you no good because then the image will also be encrypted. When this is the case, you will have to do a logical image instead. When doing a logical disk image, you image a live computer and the resultant file will contain the data on the hard drive as seen by the computer. This gives you reduced possibilities to recover deleted files and to examine file slack, but may in some cases be your only option.

Well then, to make a disk image with FTK you can use the program FTK imager. Open FTK imager and click the add new evidence button 🔍 in the upper left corner and you will get the source selection menu seen in Fig. 6.1. In this menu, you can select to image a physical or logical drive as we just discussed. You may also select a preexisting image file for analysis or reimaging or just select the contents of a specific folder. Selecting a single folder may be useful if you are collecting data from a large computer system such as a company file server.

If you want to import a physical device you will get the menu shown in Fig. 6.2 where you will have to select the physical hard drive you want to image. Selecting a logical device will give you the menu in Fig. 6.3 where you can select the partition you want to image. Selecting an image file or contents of a folder will let you browse for the image or folder you want to import. When you hit "Finish", the device you selected will be loaded into FTK imager and you may verify that you loaded the correct device by browsing it using the evidence tree located on the left-hand side.

The next step is to export the evidence that you loaded into FTK imager as an image file, the process is the same regardless of what type of device you imported to FTK. Right-click the device in the evidence tree and select export disk image as shown in Fig. 6.4. This will start the image creation wizard that will begin with the menu shown in Fig. 6.5.

This dialog lets you create a new image and make several settings by pressing add. Also notice that "Verify images after they are created" is checked. This is a feature that is present in most imaging software and that uses hashing to ensure that

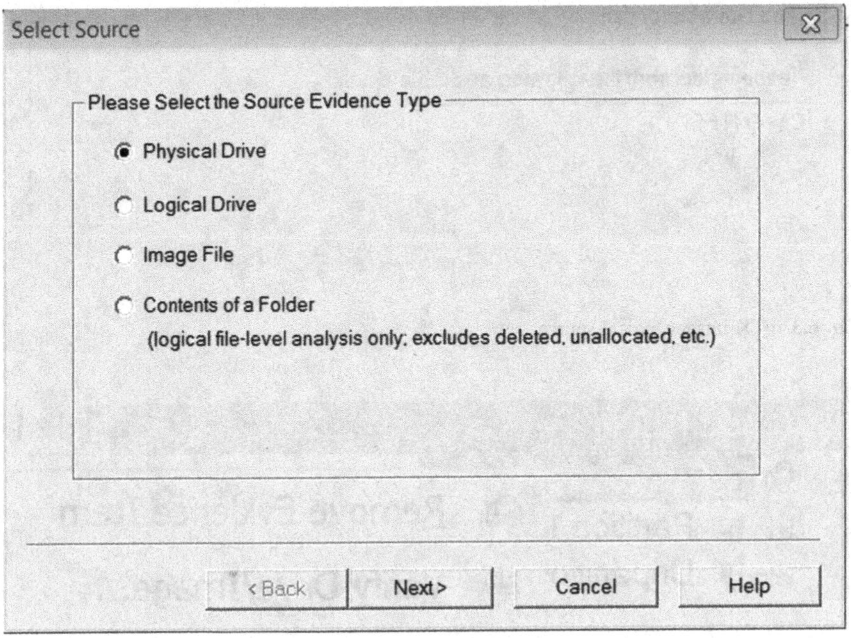

Fig. 6.1 FTK imager source selection menu

Fig. 6.2 FTK imager physical source

the image is identical to the device that is being imaged. When clicking "Add", the first step is to select the file type for the output image. The file types supported by FTK imager are DD, SMART, AFF, and E01. DD is a pure bitstream. SMART is commercial file type that is, in my experience, rarely used. AFF is an independent file format that supports encryption and compression of the output file. E01 is a proprietary format developed by Guidance Software, creator of EnCase forensics. It is arguably the most common file format, at least in law enforcement. E01 also supports compression (ForensicsWiki 2017). The "Select image type" menu is

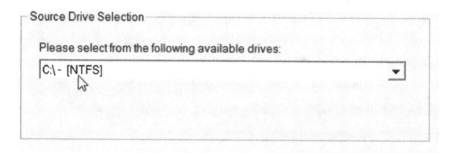

Fig. 6.3 FTK imager logical source

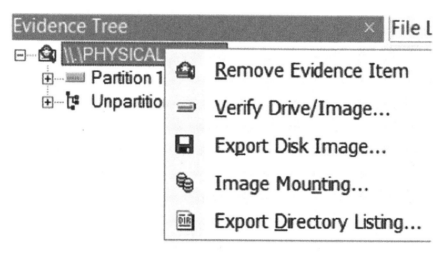

Fig. 6.4 FTK imager Export disk image

presented in Fig. 6.6. This demonstration will continue by discussing how to create an E01 image.

As shown in Fig. 6.7, it is common practice to include case data as metadata in an image. This data will help you distinguish what device and case you are working with at a later stage. The importance of this information should not be underestimated!

Finally, you need to give your image a name and set parameters for compression and fragmentation, as shown in Fig. 6.8. Compression allows you to use compression algorithms to compress the image that you create. This will slow down the process of creating the image but will also preserve space in the storage location. The image will be separated into several files, the fragmentation parameter decides the size of each file. When this is done, the image is ready to be crated. In FTK imager, you start the process by hitting "Start" in the create image menu, shown in Fig. 6.5.

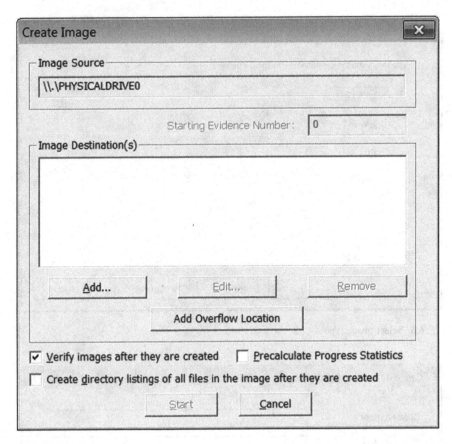

Fig. 6.5 Image creation wizard

6.2 Collecting Memory Dumps

As discussed in the theoretical section, memory can hold a lot of interesting information including encryption keys, encrypted data in its decrypted format and more. Unfortunately, the possibility to collect memory only presents itself during live investigations as the memory is volatile and the content is lost when the power is turned off. However, collecting the data in memory should be a natural part of the forensic process—whenever possible. As described by Amari (2009), the most common way to collect memory is by using some trusted tool from within the operating system of the computer from which you are going to collect the memory dump. One tool that can be used for this purpose is FTK imager. To collect a memory dump using FTK imager, begin with pressing the "Capture memory" button ▬ leading to the menu shown in Fig. 6.9. Select the destination path and filename and you are good to go! You can also select to dump the page file, where windows store volatile data that does not fit in memory.

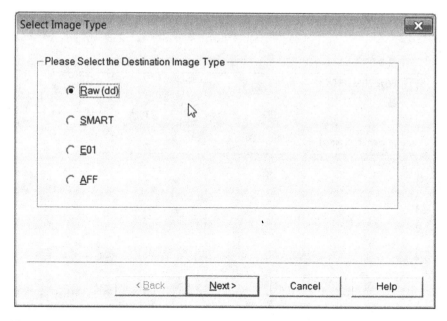

Fig. 6.6 Select image type

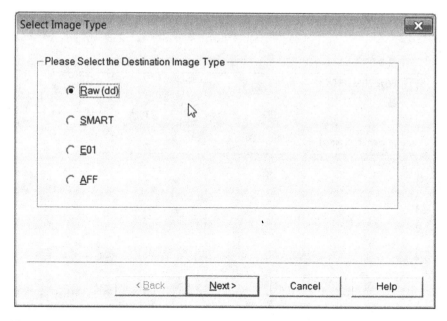

Fig. 6.7 Enter case information

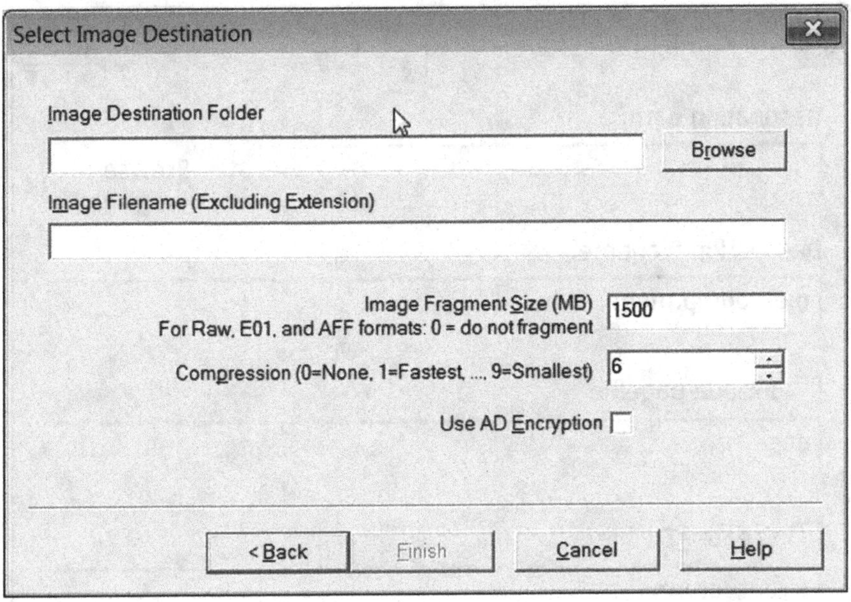

Fig. 6.8 File name, compression, and fragmentation

Important to consider when you are collecting memory is that the memory dump is stored as one big file. This fact brings that you need to ensure that the device you use to store the memory dump has a file system that can support big files. This excludes FAT32 that can only store files of 4 GB of data or less.

As described by Amari (2009), it is not always possible to access the operating system of the computer you are examining. This can, for instance, be the case when the computer is logged of and you cannot find or force the password. In these cases, there are other, more intrusive, attacks that you can use. Among those are DMA (Direct Memory Access) and cold boot attacks that will be briefly presented next.

DMA attacks exploit the design of the IEEE 1394 interface (often referred to as Firewire), more specifically the part of the standard called DMA (Witherden 2010). Many different connectors, including Firewire, Thunderbolt, PC card, and other PCI express devise, use the IEEE 1394 interface and are thereby susceptible to a DMA attack. To conduct a DMA attack, you would connect your computer to the victim computer and present your computer as a SBP—2 unit directory. The victim computer will then give you read/write access to the lower 4 GB of its RAM, allowing you to dump it (Break & Enter 2017). One tool that allows you to do a DMA attack is Inception, a free open source tool (Break & Enter 2017). While the DMA attack is easy to carry out and rather nonintrusive, it does suffer the drawback that you would normally only get access to the lower 4 GB of RAM, and modern computers often hold much more memory. Further, it should be noticed that

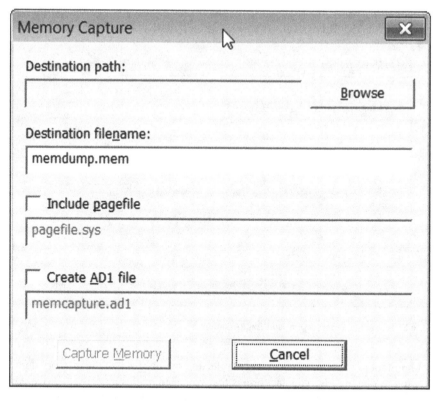

Fig. 6.9 Memory capture

operating system vendors are developing more and more defenses to the DMA attack, rendering it hard to succeed with.

Cold boot attack is an attack were you basically freeze the memory modules, reboot the victim computer and use a USB stick to make it boot a small process designed to dump the contents of memory (Halderman et al. 2009). The attack is possible due to the fact that when a computer is rebooted or turned off, data in memory is not lost immediately. Rather, it is degrading over time and the time that the data remains in memory is increased if the memory modules are cooled down. That makes it possible to boot the victim computer using a USB stick containing special software that only serves the purpose of capturing the contents of memory. It should also be noted that the attack can be successful even if the memory modules are not cooled down. While this attack can get the full content of the memory, it should be noted that it is more intrusive than the other ways of collecting memory. This is because it does require a restart of the victim computer and, in some cases, modifications in BIOS to make the victim computer boot from a USB stick.

6.3 Collecting Registry Data

The Windows registry is, as discussed, a good source of information about settings and usage of the computer you are analyzing. To analyze the registry, you need to collect the registry hives. Collecting the registry hives is a straight forward process. If you are examining the forensic image of a computer, the registry hives are stored as files in the system partition. They are located in the folder "C:\Windows \System32\config\". Also notice that NTuser.dat is located in the root of each user's home directory. If you are doing a live examination, you can extract registry files using FTK imager. Begin with pressing the button ▇. This will result in the menu seen in Fig. 6.10. In this menu, you can select if you want all registry files needed for password recovery or all registry files available. In my experience, there is no reason for selecting anything other than obtaining all registry files. This is a fairly fast process. Decide where you want to store the obtained files and press "OK".

Fig. 6.10 Capture registry files

6.4   Collecting Video from Surveillance

While not totally "on topic" for this book, collecting video from surveillance deserves a mention in this chapter because it is not as easy as you would think. What I want to mention in this brief section is that you never know what to expect when you set out to collect video from surveillance equipment. As a brief introduction to the area, know that there are loads of different manufacturers, standards, and approaches to record and store surveillance video. The lesson to learn here is to always come prepared.

In this sense, remember that some systems are only able to read FAT32 formatted memory sticks. However, other systems may store the video in files that are too big for the FAT 32 file system and in these cases you will need a memory stick formatted with NTFS or sometimes even ext4. Lesson here is to come prepared so that you can handle whatever situation that you encounter. In my personal experience, I collected video from devices that could just accept an external hard drive and devices that you could not export video from at all, instead we had to make a recording of the screen.

When you are working with video from surveillance equipment, time is usually of importance. However, you should know that it is not possible to trust the timestamp or time settings that are present in the surveillance equipment. Anyone who is used to work with surveillance video will attest to the fact that time stamps in these videos are very often way off. For that reason, you should make sure that whenever you are collecting surveillance video, note the time that is given by the surveillance gear and the current accurate time. Finally, calculate the difference if there is any.

6.5   Questions and Tasks

Here are the questions for this chapter.

1. Image some small device such as a USB drive. Create two different images using different compression settings. What are the results?
2. Collect memory from your own computer.
3. Collect the registry hives from your local computer.
4. Optional: Do a cold boot attack and describe the process!

References

Amari, K. (2009). Techniques and tools for recovering and analyzing data from volatile memory. *SANS Institute InfoSec Reading Room.*

Break & Enter. (2017). Inception. Available online: http://www.breaknenter.org/projects/inception/ [Fetched: 2017-06-03].

ForensicsWiki. (2017). Forensic File Formats. Available online: http://www.forensicswiki.org/wiki/Category:Forensics_File_Formats [Fetched: 2017-06-03].

Halderman, J. A., Schoen, S. D., Heninger, N., Clarkson, W., Paul, W., Calandrino, J. A., et al. (2009). Lest we remember: cold-boot attacks on encryption keys. *Communications of the ACM*, *52*(5), 91–98.

Witherden, F. (2010). Memory forensics over the ieee 1394 interface. Available online: https://freddie.witherden.org/pages/ieee-1394-forensics/revisions/c1c615827b7647933e5a3d00668d6183.pdf [Fetched: 2017-06-03].

Chapter 7
Indexing, Searching, and Cracking

Abstract When working as a forensic examiner, it is not uncommon to encounter encrypted files or entire partitions. When that is the case, the encrypted data must be decrypted in order for the forensic expert to be able to examine it. A tool that can be used to launch attacks against encrypted data is AccessData Password Recovery ToolKit (PRTK). This chapter provides a practical guide on how to use PRTK to decrypt encrypted data. Further, this chapter discusses two different ways of searching, live search and index search. A live search is just a search over the entire device you are examining for a keyword or pattern. An index search on the other hand is based on a pre-created index containing all strings on the device. The strings are mapped to their location. An index search can be much faster than a live search but depends and is limited by the way the index was generated. For that reason, this chapter also includes a description of different index settings in AccessData FTK.

Keywords Indexing · Searching · Decryption · PRTK

This chapter is devoted to actions that are commonly carried out before you get into searching for artifacts. It covers three common tasks in forensic examinations that are more general in nature compared to looking for a specific type of data. As in the rest of Sect. 7.2, hands on examples are provided using Accessdata tools. However, the methods can be used in similar ways using tools from other vendors.

7.1 Indexing

Indexing is a technique where you create an index of a forensic image. When creating an index, the data on the hard drive is seen in alphanumeric form. The data is read from beginnings to end and all cohesive strings are listed in the index. You will commonly also get a list of strings that belong to each file. The resulting index is useful in two ways; first you can use the index to do fast searches for keywords. This is because the index contains information that states were each found string is

© The Author(s) 2017

J. Kävrestad, *Guide to Digital Forensics*, SpringerBriefs in Computer Science,
https://doi.org/10.1007/978-3-319-67450-6_7

‡ ·$ ·Đÿ ·Stretch=ÿ$ ·Èÿ ·Center=ÿ$ ·Ñÿ ·5¤þ · ·çÿè · · ·‡FF808080$ ·æÿ ·0.5,0.75,0.5,0.75qÿ · ·

Fig. 7.1 Data sample

located. Thus, if you search for a keyword the forensic software will return all files that contains that keyword. The second use of the index is as a word list in password cracking. Since the index will contain every alphanumeric string present on the device that you are examining, there is a good chance that it will contain one or more passwords related to something on the system.

On the topic of indexes, there are some terms that you need to be familiar with; spaces, letters, and noise words. Spaces are symbols that are used to separate the data into strings, letters are the symbols that make up a string, and noise words are words that are ignored in the index because they are considered too frequent. Noise words are usually words such as "it", "and", and "or". As an example of how the indexing works, consider a case when the signs a–z are considered letters and all other sign are considered spaces. Then, look at the data sample in Fig. 7.1.

The strings that will be added to the index are the following:

1. Stretch
2. Center
3. FF

The reason is that those strings are the cohesive strings of signs, which are defined as letters in the sample data. If numbers were to be defined as letters, the third string would be FF808080 and if center was to be added as a noise word, it would not be added to the index. It is also common that forensic tools allow for the opportunity to limit the string length for index entries and other fine tuning. In FTK, creating an index is done during preprocessing (as described in Chap. 10) or by hitting "Evidence" and then "Additional analysis" and selecting "Search Index" under the "Index/Tools tab". Note that you may only modify letters, noise words, and such when creating the index as a preprocessing task. The index settings window is demonstrated in Fig. 7.2. To add or remove symbols or words in sections, simply use the add or remove buttons. Understanding the indexing process is crucial in order to fully be able to use the index. For instance, when using the index for password cracking, you must ensure that characters you expect in the password are not considered spaces in the indexing process. Further, those signs must be added as letters to be added to the index.

As final notes on indexing, you should know that creating an index is a time-consuming process. However, searching for keywords with an index is much faster than searching a case without an index. Also, the index is very useful for password cracking. You should also know that the index will include words that are readable to the indexing software at the time of indexing. If you, for instance, consider a case where you are examining an image that contains a compressed folder which contains a lot of text files, you create the index before you expand the compressed folder. In this case, the text from the files in the compressed folder will

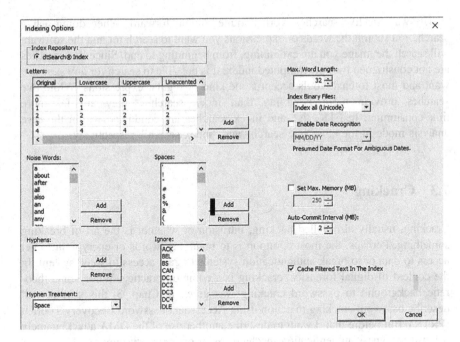

Fig. 7.2 FTK indexing options

not be present in the index; this is because it was in a compressed format at the time of indexing. The same case applies to encrypted files and, while not a bug, must be understood by the forensic examiner. That being said, indexes are very useful for the forensic expert who knows how and when to use them!

7.2 Searching

A very common task during forensic examinations is to search for keywords. In my experience, searching for different keywords is of interest in almost every case. While searching is a common and important task, it can be time-consuming and it is therefore important to get its right. Most forensic tools, including FTK, provide two different ways to conduct searches, namely live and index searches. An index search is a search through an index. If the word you are searching for is present in the index, you will get a hit. The main advantage of the index search is that it is very fast; you commonly get the results instantly. However, as made evident by the discussion on indexing, it is hard to find strings that contain signs which were not considered letters during the indexing process. Further, it can be difficult to find sentences even if many index search engines allow the use of regular expressions and logical operators.

The way the live searches work is quite straight forward. When doing a live search, you submit the words or expressions you want to search for and the software will search the image you are examining, from beginning to end. Since live searches are not constrained by a precomputed index, it is possible to search for any sign you want and most forensic tools accept some kind of regular expressions. While live searches provide more flexibility than index searches, they are far more time-consuming. In FTK, live and index searches are conducted within the case analysis mode in the tabs "live search" and "index search", respectively.

7.3 Cracking

Cracking, usually also called hacking, intrusion or whatnot is the art of breaking something. Perhaps, the most common is to break passwords or encryption to get access to data or to break authentication systems to gain access to some system. In the context of digital forensics, cracking is a common practice. While some theoretic background to password cracking was given in Chap. 3, this section will describe password cracking in action using Accessdata Password Recovery ToolKit (PRTK). But before that, I want to describe another use of the DMA attack, namely using it to bypass authentication mechanisms of operating systems.

Remember that the DMA attack is possible because you can connect to the Firewire port of a target computer and get read/write access to the lower 4 GB of memory. Most operating systems keep code that handles the login procedure in memory and the code (very abstracted) says that if you submit the correct password, you are in. Else, you are out. The tool Inception, discussed in the previous section on DMA attacks, can search for this code and modify it so that you are in no matter what password you submit. Using this attack let us you log into an operating system without submitting the correct password. Thus, it is a very powerful tool to use during a live investigation where you would need access to the target computer to collect volatile data.

Using this approach to crack your way into a computer has been very successful in the past. In my own experience, it has worked wonder against Windows as well as MAC. However, while the attack is still possible, it is less likely to succeed today. This is for two reasons. First, modern computers usually have more than 4 GB or memory and for the attack to work, the authentication code must be present in the part of memory that Inception can access. Second, more and more protections against DMA attacks are created and implemented by operating system vendors, hardware manufacturers, and third-party developers. However, the attack remains relevant as it is often the only way to break into a live system without a reboot.

As for password cracking using PRTK, PRTK is a tool that can crack a large number of different file types and encryption schemes. However, as discussed in the theoretical section, perhaps, the most important part of password cracking is the engine for developing dictionaries. On this topic, PRTK does a good job. When you find some encrypted file or password you need to crack, you can summarize the procedure you need to follow as follows:

1. Create dictionaries;
2. Create attack profile;
3. Run the attack

To begin, an overview of PRTK is shown in Fig. 7.3. The main left pane lists all waiting jobs and marking a job will show details of that job in the right pane. You can also double click a job to see more detailed information and progress about it. The tools menu is used to access the dictionary tool and the edit menu is used to access the profile creation menu.

To create dictionaries, enter the dictionary tool as shown in Fig. 7.4. This is the tool you would use to import a dictionary that is in the form of a simple row-separated text file. This would be the case if you downloaded password lists from the Internet or if you exported a case index. This tool also provides options to remove duplicates, remove long or short words, and choose what characters to include. When you selected your settings, hit generate to generate the list.

To create a biographical dictionary, there is a special tool accessible through the dictionary tools menu. There are also tools for passphrases and permutations of words; all three tools work in similar ways. The tool for creating biographical lists is shown in Fig. 7.5. What you should do is to input the biographical data you found. The words can be categorized according to its type, such as name, date, or plain words. When you entered all the data you found, you can go to the generator tab and hit generate. PRTK will combine the different words and dates, and create a

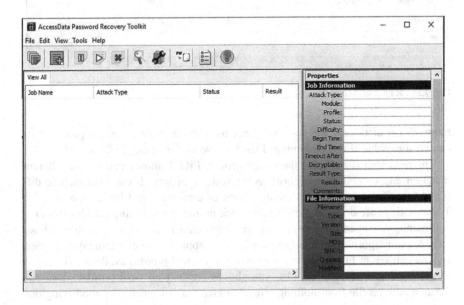

Fig. 7.3 PRTK interface overview

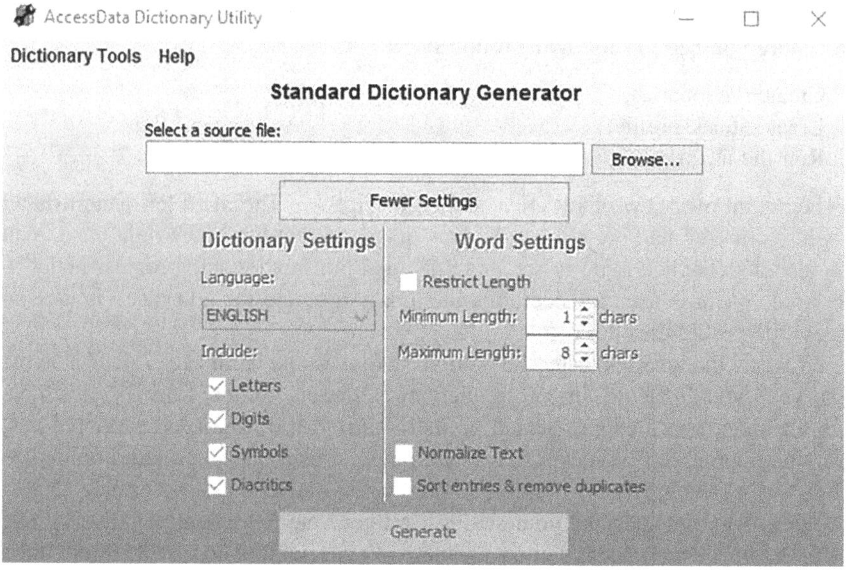

Fig. 7.4 PRTK dictionary tool

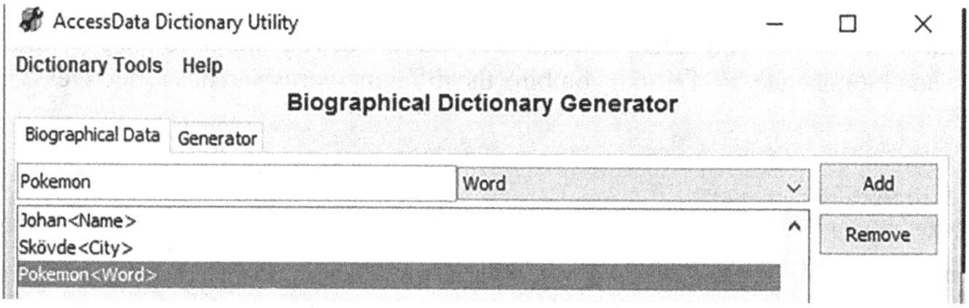

Fig. 7.5 PRTK bio dictionary tool

biographical dictionary for you. Note that the dictionary creation is a process that can be somewhat time-consuming. Plan your work for optimal efficiency!

The next step is to create the attack profile. PRTK allows you to run different mutation and combination algorithms on your dictionary. It can also include different brute force attacks and combinations of dictionary and brute force attacks. These settings are done by creating an attack profile. By selecting profiles from the edit menu, you open the profile manager, presented in Fig. 7.6. A profile is basically a set of algorithms, called rules, which are applied to one or more dictionaries. As you can see in Fig. 7.6, there are some pre-created profiles available. However, to get good and efficient attacks, you should create your own profiles. You can create a new profile from nothing (New) or create a new profile by modifying one

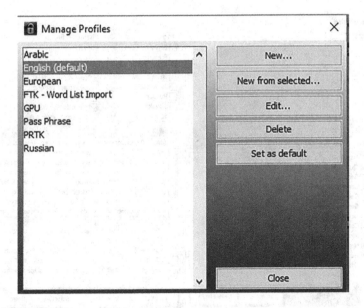

Fig. 7.6 Profile manager

of the existings (New from selected). Settings for your new profile are configured in the profile configuration tool shown in Fig. 7.7. All dictionaries that you ever imported into PRTK are listed to the left. There are also some default dictionaries in different languages. Select the dictionaries that should be used in your profile. Then hit the order tab to select the order in which the dictionaries should be applied. The available rules are listed to the right. Simply check the rules you want to use and notice that the order they appear in is the order that they will run in. I want to mention the highlighted rule. This is the rule that tests every entry in every dictionary. There are other rules that test the words in the dictionary as upper or lower case only. Also, notice that the rules are marked BAS or ADV. BAS is for basic and those rules are less time-consuming than ADV rules. The first number in the BAS and ADV marking also indicates the complexness of a rule. As such, ADV-2-1 is more complex than ADV-1-2 and thus, more time-consuming. When your profile is completed select OK to save it.

The final step in the attack process is to execute the actual attack. To begin, drop the file you want to crack into PRTK. PRTK will analyze the file and try to figure out the file type and suggest the type of attack to use. You can read about all different attack types that PRTK can execute through the user manual accessible by clicking the question mark in the main program. When the file is analyzed, PRTK will present the wizard shown in Fig. 7.8. This is when you select the profile to use for the attack. This is done in the upper left corner. It is possible to create new profiles from here. Clicking next will take you to the list of available attacks as demonstrated in Fig. 7.9. In this case, the file to be attacked a password protected .rar file. It is only possible to do a dictionary attack against this type of files but

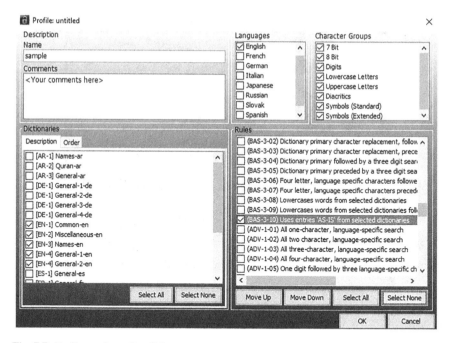

Fig. 7.7 Profile configuration dialog

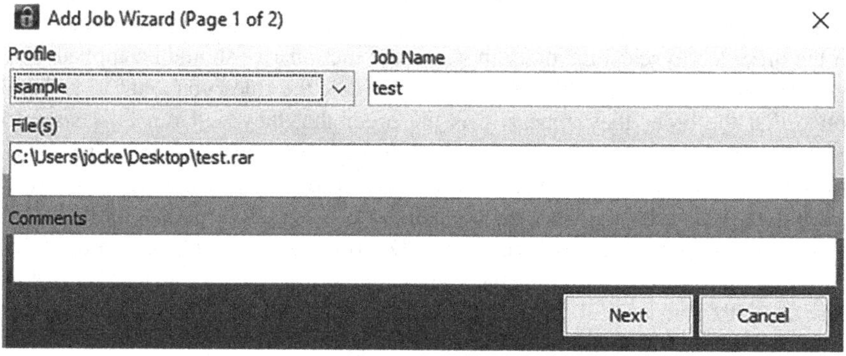

Fig. 7.8 Add job wizard

there are files that have several different attack options. Select the one you want to use and hit Finish to start the attack.

When the attack is started, you can see the status of the attack (Queued, running, and finished) from the PRTK main window. If you double click an attack, you can see detailed progression statistics including what rule PRTK is currently working with and how many attempts that PRTK can make per second. Note that different

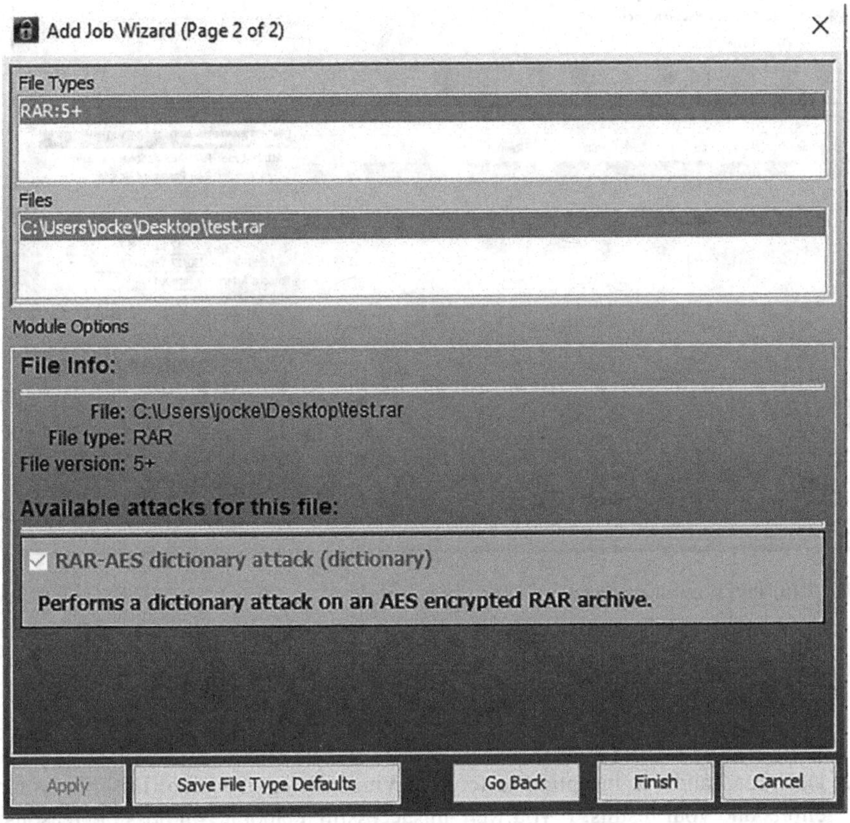

Fig. 7.9 Select attack

file types have vastly different attack times. When the attack is complete, PRTK will show you the password in the right part of the main window, as demonstrated in Fig. 7.10. At times, the password is followed by an "*". This indicates that PRTK found several passwords. You can see all of them by double clicking the attack.

7.4 Questions and Tasks

Here are the questions for this chapter.

1. Index a forensic image and then search for the following keywords. Do live and index searches for all keywords. Describe the results of the searches and explain why differences may appear.

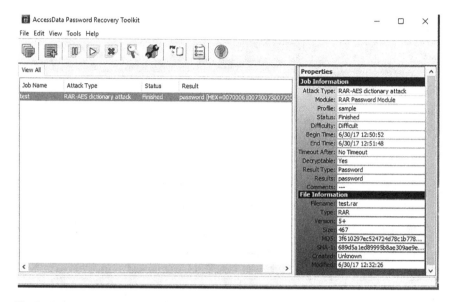

Fig. 7.10 PRTK result presentation

    a. System32
    b. .appdata
    c. Alink.dll

2. Download and use inception to force a Windows logon screen. Describe your efforts and your results. If you were unsuccessful, elaborate on possible reasons for why.
3. Create a password protected RAR archive and use your favorite password cracker to crack it open. Describe your efforts and your results.

Chapter 8
Finding Artifacts

Abstract While it is impossible to describe all possible artifacts that may be of interest in any given investigation, this chapter aims to describe how to find some artifacts that are very common to look for. The chapter first describes how to find information such as install date and time zone settings from the Windows registry. Next, the chapter provides a rather detailed description of how to analyze a partition table in order to ensure that all drive space is allocated to a partition. An overview of how to search for deleted files is also included. A lot of good information can be found in file metadata, which includes information such as when a file was created and by who. Analyzing different kinds of metadata is described before the chapter presents an approach on how to analyze log files. The end of this chapter is a discussion on how to analyze unorganized data such as unpartitioned disk space or slack.

Keywords Metadata · Windows registry · Partition analysis

In doing a forensic examination to answer questions asked by the investigation, you need to look for evidence that you can use to draw conclusions. The pieces of evidence that you find are sometimes referred to as artifacts, and this chapter will describe how to find some artifacts that are common for a forensic examiner to look for. This chapter will also present demonstrations of how to analyze file metadata, log files, chat logs, and unorganized data such as slack.

8.1 Install Date

The install date for the computer can be of great importance. Consider a situation where you are looking for information about some event that took place in 2015. If the computer was installed in 2016, that information will be hard to come by. Further, if a suspect says that he or she just bought the computer, in 2017, but it was installed in 2015, it is easy to suspect that the suspect is hiding something. Anyhow,

© The Author(s) 2017
J. Kävrestad, *Guide to Digital Forensics*, SpringerBriefs in Computer Science,
https://doi.org/10.1007/978-3-319-67450-6_8

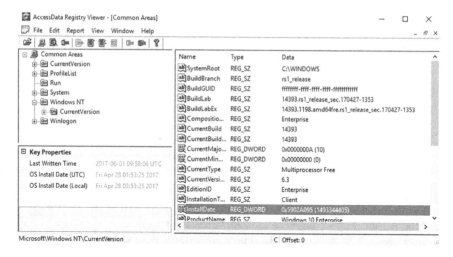

Fig. 8.1 Install date in Windows registry

the install date is found in Windows registry, in the system hive. Using AccessData registry viewer, the install date can be found by viewing common areas, as seen in Fig. 8.1.

As displayed, the InstallDate key holds the value describing when the system was installed. The date is expressed as a UNIX timestamp but registry viewer presents a translated timestamp in the bottom left pane. Note that the timestamp is reported with the local time zone and UTC. Time zones are discussed in more detail in the next section. The InstallDate key can also be found by browsing the registry hive to the following path: Microsoft\Windows NT\CurrentVersion.

8.2 Time Zone Information

As you are surely familiar with, the world is divided into time zones that make the time differ from location to location. The time zone settings on your computer will therefore affect the displayed time and the time that is noted in timestamps. For that reason, it is important to verify the time zone settings (as well as the correctness of the system clock) during a forensic examination. Basically, the time zone will create a time offset from UTC. That is, how much the system clock will differ from UTC (sometimes also called Greenwich Mean Time). The time zone is sometimes expressed as the name of the time zone (Pacific Standard Time) or as the offset from UTC (UTC-08:00). A complete reference of all time zones and offsets is present in Chap. 16. Time zone settings are found in Windows registry, in the following path: ControlSet001\Control\TimeZoneInformation. Figure 8.2 shows time zone information found with registry viewer common areas.

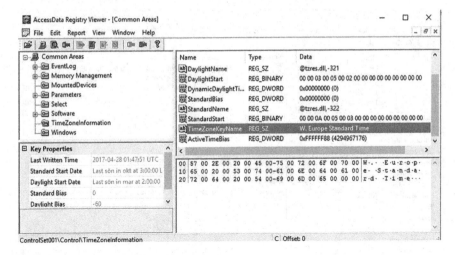

Fig. 8.2 Time zone in Registry viewer

The system clock is also dependent on the daylight savings settings. Daylight savings tells you to turn the clock one hour back in the fall and one hour forward in the spring. The dates when daylight savings are applied are also found in the different keys in ControlSet001\Control\TimeZoneInformation.

8.3   Users on the System

Finding out what users that are present on the system is a task that is sometimes overlooked. I must admit, this is a task that I have personally overlooked at several occasions. The thing is that a suspect may decide to claim that some other user did everything that the prosecutor claims that he did. If this statement is presented in court and the forensic examiner cannot testify to whether or not there were any other users present on the computer, this may harm the case. There are several ways to find out what users that are present on the system such as looking into what users have home folders in the Users folder. However, it is easy to manipulate a file system. Thus, looking into the registry is a much safer way to find out the users of the system. Information about the users on the system is present in the SAM hive under the key: SAM\SAM\Domains\Account\Users. Each user gets a key of its own, and clicking each key will show you information about the user. An example is given in Fig. 8.3, showing information about the administrator user. This is a good place to describe user identifiers in Windows. Each user is given an SID (Security Identifier), and the last part of the SID is a numeric value called a relative identifier (RID). The RID for the built-in administrator account is always 500, and the guest account is always 501.

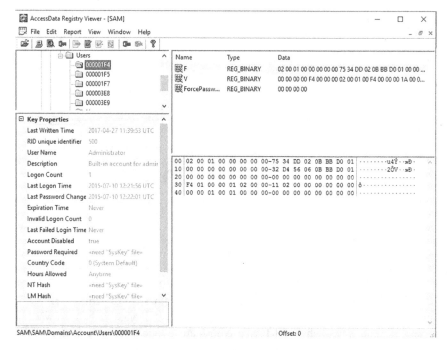

Fig. 8.3 User information in windows registry

The user accounts added manually starts at RID 1000. Notable is that the SID and RID never change for a user account. However, it is possible to change the username. As such, it is possible to change the name of the administrator account into something else and name a normal account administrator, for the sake of confusing. However, it is the SID and not the name that is used to evaluate user permissions (Zacker 2014). Also, note that users are removed are, at least for a time, kept in the registry. That being said, the SAM registry hive will tell you the users present on the systems, and AccessData Registry Viewer will evaluate the RID and username for each user. The registry will also keep track of the number of logins for each user, when the user last logged and the user last changed password and more.

8.4 Registered Owner

When installing Windows, you can register a name as the registered owner of the system and this information is kept in registry. It may seem as if someone with ill intent would make sure not to store his own name in registry, but I found the name of the suspect as the registered owner on more than one occasion. The registered owner is present in the SYSTEM registry hive at the following path: Microsoft \Windows NT\CurrentVersion.

8.5   Partition Analysis and Recovery

As discussed, accounting for all data on a hard drive is essential and a good way to identify hidden partitions or slack space. Looking at a hard drive in FTK imager, you will see the list of partitions and "Unpartitioned space" shows unallocated space on the hard drive. As shown in Fig. 8.4, the unallocated space is shown as a list of files. Each file contains a contiguous run of unallocated space and the name identifies the starting sector of the free space (AccessData 2013).

It is normal to find small pieces of unallocated space, as in the example. However, if you encounter big chunks of unallocated space it is wise to do a manual examination of the partitions on the hard drive.

When manually examining the partitions on the hard drive, we need to recall that a hard drive will, normally, contain a Master boot record (MBR) containing a list of partitions. This is what FTK (and most other forensic software) will use to make out the partitions on the hard drive. The partitions are listed in the partition table located in offset 446 in the MBR that is 446 bytes from the beginning of the MBR (Guidance Software 2016). The partition table continues until the MBR signature (hex 55 AA) is found. Each partition table record is 16 bytes long. Figure 8.5 shows the data representing a partition table with one entry. The marked part is the partition table and the MBR signature, and the underlined part is the partition table entry seen by marking the entire disk in FTK imager. In FTK imager, you can jump to a sector or byte offset by right clicking in the data field and selecting the appropriate option.

What you need to know next is how to interpret the partition table record, which is structured as follows:

- The first byte tells if the partition is bootable or not; in this case, 00 is for no, 80 is yes.
- The following three bytes tell the starting sector of the partition in CHS format.

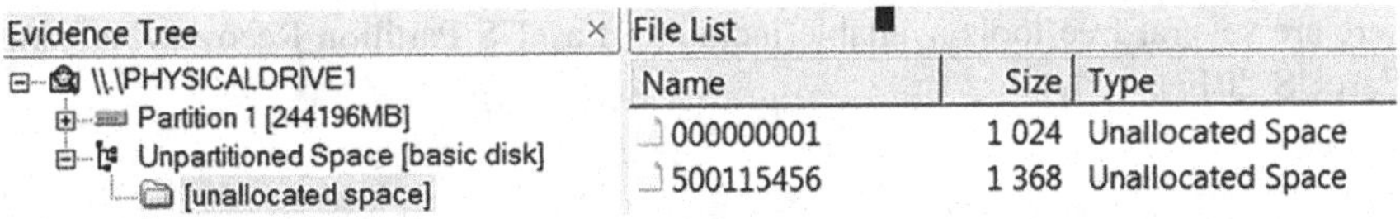

Fig. 8.4 Unallocated space shown in FTK imager

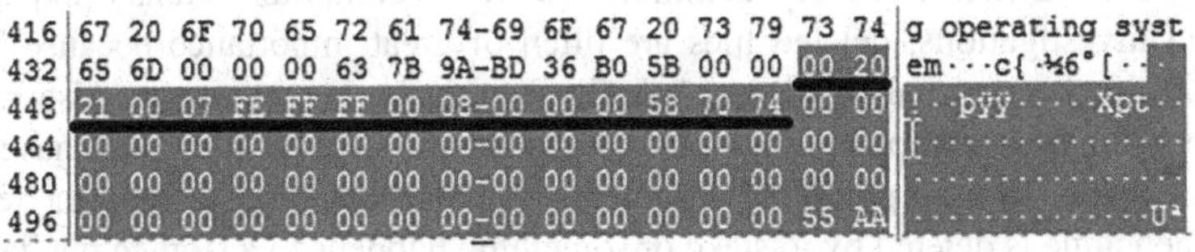

Fig. 8.5 Partition table entry viewed in FTK imager

```
EB 52 90 4E 54 46 53 20-20 20 20 00 02 08 00 00│ëR·NTFS      ·····
00 00 00 00 00 F8 00 00-3F 00 FF 00 00 08 00 00│·····ø··?·ÿ·····
00 00 00 00 80 00 80 00-FF 57 70 74 00 00 00 00│········ÿẄpt····
00 00 0C 00 00 00 00 00-02 00 00 00 00 00 00 00│|···············
F6 00 00 00 01 00 00 00-4C 2C 09 40 32 09 40 04│ö·······L,·@2·@·
```

Fig. 8.6   Start of VBR for an NTFS partition

- The following byte tells the partition type, in this case 07 for NTFS.
- The following three bytes tell the ending sector of the partition in CHS format.
- The following four bytes tell the relative sector offset, that is, how many sectors from the beginning of the disk the partition is located. The hexadecimal value in this case is 00 08 00 00 translating to 2048. Note that the byte order is little-endian. Also note that this offset is calculated in sectors and not bytes!
- The final four bytes will tell the total numbers of sectors in the partition. The hexadecimal value in this case is 00 58 70 74 translating to 1953519616. Note that the byte order is little-endian. A sector is commonly 512 bytes large making the size of this partition roughly 931 Gigabytes.

Now you know that what you need to do to find disk space not included in a partition. Namely walk the partition table and note the starting and ending sectors of each partition. Gaps that you find could be slack space but may also contain hidden partitions. To find a hidden partition, you would search the unallocated space to search for patterns indicating a volume boot record (VBR), which is present in the start of a partition. For instance, a VBR belonging to an NTFS partition will begin with hexadecimal EB 52 90 4E 54 46 53 as shown in Fig. 8.6.

Located at offset 40 (40 bytes from the start) of the VBR is 8 bytes indicating the size of the partition, as shown in the marked part of Fig. 8.5. The byte order is little-endian. At this point, you can evaluate if the partition size seems to match the size of the partitions found in the partition table. If not, you may find a hidden partition that you can recover. Unfortunately, FTK does not do a good job at recovering partitions. However, EnCase forensics is great at partition recovery and there are several free tools available including EaseUS Partition Recovery Wizard (EaseUS 2017).

8.6   Deleted Files

Finding deleted files is a very common task for a computer forensic expert. In criminal investigations, deleted files are often of great importance because, well, criminals like to cover their tracks. Actually, criminals, just as anyone else, delete files to keep their computers nice and clean and the deleted files may have evidentiary value. In a corporate environment, it is also common to recover deleted files when a file is deleted by mistake or something happens to a storage media. The process of recovering deleted files is usually called data recovery and can be done in a number of different ways. This rest of this chapter will discuss data recovery in the following three ways:

- Recovering files deleted from the MFT,
- File carving, and
- Recover data fragments.

Recovering data fragments is done using the approach discussed in the ending section of this chapter. The remainder of this section will introduce "Recovering files deleted from MFT" and "'File carving".

8.6.1 Recovering Files Deleted from MFT

Remember that Windows systems commonly use the NTFS file system and that all files are listed in the Master File Table (MFT). What happens when a file is deleted is that the file entry in the MFT is removed but the actual file is commonly left on the hard drive. The file is left until it is overwritten. Files deleted in this manner can be restored by searching the sectors in the partition for sectors holding files not present in the MFT. Since the file is not actually gone, the restoration process is simple. This process can be completed using tools available online and is commonly performed automatically by forensic tools. Actually, this process is completed by FTK and FTK imager.

8.6.2 File Carving

File carving is used to find files that cannot just be restored. Reason for why a file cannot be restored can be that pointers to where the file is located have been broken; the file may be partially overwritten or located in some unorganized area such as the page file. As discussed in Chap. 3, different file types contain specific data that distinguish them from files of other types. It is common for a file to have a header, in the beginning of the file, containing a file signature and a trailer at the end of the file. Thus, if you find the file signature and the trailer, everything in between should be a part of the file. This is how file carving works. When carving for files you are searching for file signatures and trailers and try to rebuild the files.

File carving is usually done using a file carver. A file carver is a tool that does the carving process. Depending on what type of material you are carving for, there are different tools of different qualities. However, most forensic softwares include some type of data carving functionality. In FTK, you can do data carving during preprocessing or by hitting "Evidence" and then "Additional analysis" and selecting "Data carve". Hitting the "Carving options", you notice that there are several file types that FTK can carve for. There is also the option to create a custom carver. If you find yourself working a case with special file types, you may want to create a

```
000000 25 50 44 46 2D 31 2E 34-0D 25 E2 E3 CF D3 0D 0A   %PDF-1.4 ·$ââÏÓ··
000016 34 20 30 20 6F 62 6A 0D-3C 3C 2F 4C 69 6E 65 61   4 0 obj ·<</Linea
000032 72 69 7A 65 64 20 31 2F-4C 20 35 30 31 35 32 37   rized 1/L 501527
000048 2F 4F 20 36 2F 45 20 34-39 38 31 31 31 2F 4E 20   /O 6/E 498111/N
000064 31 2F 54 20 35 30 31 33-32 38 2F 48 20 5B 20 34   1/T 501328/H [ 4
```

Fig. 8.7 Partial header of a PDF

custom carver. In doing this, you have to determine the file signature and the offset where the file signature begins. Consider the header of a PDF file in Fig. 8.7. The file signature is "%PDF-1.4" and it is located at the beginning of the file; thus it is located at offset 0. However, if the file signature was just "PDF-1.4", it would have been located at offset 1, one character in, counting from the beginning of the file. Note that the offset in this example is counted in bytes.

When you established a file signature, you need to decide how the file ends. Some files have a fixed length and then you can state the file size. Other files may have an ending signature or tag that you can input.

When you are working with data carving, there are some things to consider. First of all, the number of false positives (found files that are not really files) is often large. This is because there can be a lot of file headers lingering in slack, pagefile, and so on. Those headers will likely result in a false result being produced. While you need to be aware of this issue, the risk of creating false evidence is extremely small, negligible even. For a carver to generate a file that can be used as evidence, it has to be

1. a working complete file and
2. fit into the active case.

The chance of a file matching the above criteria's being a false hit is, in my opinion, impossible.

What you also need to consider when working with data carving is that the chance of the carved files being altered is not negligible. It is very possible that some bits are missing from the original file resulting with the fact that the carved file differs from the original. A few missing bits are often not even visible but can, at times, modify important data such as timestamps. If some part of a carved file is messed up, this is commonly obvious. However, when drawing conclusions, one could argue that you should be a little bit extra careful when drawing conclusions based on carved files.

8.7 Analyzing Compound Files

Several files that can contain important data are so-called compound files. A compound file is basically a file that maintains its own file structure and includes file types such as compressed files and Microsoft office files. In the case of compressed files, the file content is not readable when the file is in the compressed state. Before a proper analysis or a compound file can be conducted, it has to be unpacked or expanded. This process makes all the content of the file visible to the examiner and the forensic software.

Just to be clear, it is commonly not possible to search or overview the analyzed compound files, compressed files in particular, manually or automatically before they are unpacked. Knowing this is especially important during preprocessing, because if you do not unpack compound files during preprocessing, most preprocessing tasks will not apply to the contents of the compound files. However, expanding compound files can be a time-consuming task. To expand compound files in FTK, select "Expand compound files" during preprocessing or at a later stage as additional analysis.

8.8 Analyzing File Metadata

As been discussed over and over again, all files contain metadata and metadata is information about the file it regards. While it is easy to focus on the actual file content, metadata is often of equal interest to a forensic examiner. What information that is present in the metadata is highly dependent on file type. However, most file systems attach some metadata, including timestamps, to all files in the file system. In FTK, you can view the metadata of a file by marking the file and then hit the properties tab in the view pane, as shown in Fig. 8.8.

The remainder of this section will discuss the following types of metadata, commonly of interest to a forensic examiner:

- NTFS timestamps,
- Exif data,
- Office metadata.

Properties	
Name	file1.txt
Item Number	2002
File Type	7 bit text
Path	test [AD1]/file1.txt
⊟ General Info	
⊞ File Size	
⊟ File Dates	
Date Created	2017-06-27 16:09:57 (2017-06-27 14:09:57 UTC)
Date Accessed	2017-06-27 16:09:57 (2017-06-27 14:09:57 UTC)
Date Modified	2017-06-27 16:11:03 (2017-06-27 14:11:03 UTC)
⊟ File Attributes	

Fig. 8.8 View metadata in FTK

8.8.1 NTFS Timestamps

All files created on an NTFS file system gets timestamps and the timestamps can tell you a fair bit about what happened to a file. The timestamps present on a file on an NTFS file system are the following (Knutsson 2016):

- Created, indicating when the file was created on the system;
- Modified, indicating when the file was last modified;
- Accessed, indicating when the file was last read;
- MFT modified time, indicating when the file metadata was last modified.

Reading the timestamps will give you a good indication of when a file was created, last accessed, and modified. However, you should know that the created timestamp gets updated at every occurrence that the file is created. Created in this context includes when it is moved to a computer, when it is originally created and if it is cut and pasted. All of those actions will also update the Accessed record. However, the Modified record seems to accurately describe when the file was last modified.

It is also important to know that there are actually two sets of timestamps related to each file on the NTFS file system (Rusbarsky 2012). Many tools used to confuse forensic examiners will only change one set of timestamps and enable a forensic examiner to analyze the timestamps to find discrepancies. If there are discrepancies in the sets of timestamps, it is a sure sign that someone is trying to hide something.

8.8.2 Exif Data

Pictures usually contain a very extensive set of metadata called Exif (Exchangeable image file format) data. Exif data is often a very rich source of information even if the precise nature of the data is up to the camera vendor. The Exif data can tell you a lot about a picture and how it was taken including the following:

- Name of the device taking the picture;
- Serial number of the device taking the picture;
- Version and model of the device taking the picture;
- GPS coordinates describing where the picture was taken;
- Custom tags added by the camera vendor or person taking the photo;
- Much more.

While FTK can be used to read Exif data, there are several tools freely available. A personal favorite is the Exif tool by Phil Harvey, available for download at http://www.sno.phy.queensu.ca/~phil/exiftool/. To ensure that FTK displays all Exif data, be sure to check the "Meta carve" option during preprocessing, or hit "Evidence", then "Additional analysis" and select "Meta carve".

8.8.3 Office Metadata

As described by SoftXpantion (2009), Microsoft office files come with a lot of metadata that can be of great interest to a computer forensic examiner. The office metadata holds several pieces of information including the following:

- Name of original author;
- Name of the person who last saves the document;
- Original creation date;
- Last saved date;
- When the document was last printed;
- Total time spent working on the document.

The name recorded in the office metadata is the name that the user submitted for the first time when office was started. It is easy to input your real name without afterthoughts and then never think of it again, thus office metadata can be an invaluable source of information for a computer forensic expert. Office metadata can be read by right clicking a document and going to the properties tab. The metadata can also be seen in FTK, as previously described in Fig. 8.8 or by right clicking a file in Windows and selecting the details tab, as shown in Fig. 8.9.

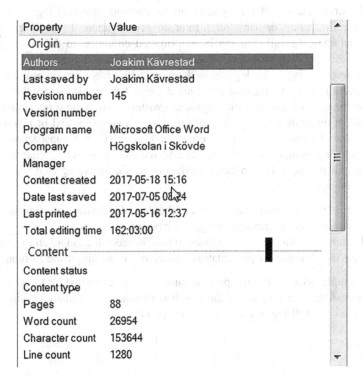

Fig. 8.9 Office file metadata seen in Windows

8.9   Analyzing Log Files

In a computer forensic examination, it is common to analyze how different applications were used. This can, for instance, include messages going in and out of a chat application or analyzing transactions to and from a bit coin wallet. There are some tools available that can analyze data from some applications automatically but it is, in my own experience, equally common that you need to analyze application log files in order to establish how an application was used. The rest of this section provides an example of an approach that can be used to analyze chat logs; the approach can also be applied to application logs.

Analyzing chat logs is commonly a quite straight forward process as the structure of chat logs tends to be rather obvious. As any log files, chat logs come in many different forms and it is of high importance that you get an understanding of how the particulate log file works. While it is often quite easy to figure out the structure of a chat log, there are more complicated examples and if you do not fully understand a chat log by looking at it, it is encouraged to conduct an experiment to understand the workings of the chat program in question.

When you understand the chat log, you are commonly tasked with transferring the chat log into a format that is easier to read for the investigator. In some cases, you are asked to provide a summary including parts of the chat log and in other cases, the investigator will want you to submit the complete chat log. To comply with the transparency demand on a forensic investigation, I would encourage always including the full chat log in unformatted condition to the investigation. However, this does not include a reformatted version or a summary.

While reformatting a chat log can be done manually, it is often times much more time-efficient to reformat the chat log using a script. By writing a script that fetches the interesting data from each message and rewrites it into a more readable format you create a time-efficient way of working. Using a script instead of manual formatting also decreases the risk of errors and increases the consistency. Also, whenever using homemade tools, be sure to mention that fact in your report to maintain transparency! To summarize, this process for analyzing chat logs can be summarized as follows:

- Use your favorite forensic tool to locate chat logs. Common search terms would, for instance, include message, msg, received, or sent.
- Understand the chat log by examining it and, if needed, conduct an experiment.
- Prepare the chat log for presentation, preferably in an automatic fashion.

As an example, let us apply the process on a chat log generated by the chat client called jitsi. A snippet containing the two first messages of a jitsi chat log is presented below (A full log is presented in Chap. 17):

```
<?xml version=''1.0'' encoding=''UTF-8'' standalone=''no''?>
<history>
   <record timestamp=''2017-06-27T13:16:07.826+0200''>
      <dir>in</dir>
      <msg><![CDATA[zup_]]></msg>
      <msgTyp>text/plain</msgTyp>
      <enc>UTF-8</enc>
      <uid>149856217370418137890</uid>
      <receivedTimestamp>2017-06-27T13:16:07.260
+0200</receivedTimestamp>
   </record>
   <record timestamp=''2017-06-27T13:16:21.179+0200''>
      <dir>out</dir>
      <msg><![CDATA[kollar lite affärer....sj?]]></msg>
      <msgTyp>text/plain</msgTyp>
      <enc>UTF-8</enc>
      <uid>149856218114519064878</uid>
      <receivedTimestamp>2017-06-27T13:16:21.149
+0200</receivedTimestamp>
   </record>
```

Looking at the chat log, with the intent of finding time for the message, receiving or sending users and the message content, let us conclude the following:

- Each message begins with the tag <record> and ends with the tag </record>.
- Time of the message is included in the starting record tag, there is also a received timestamp that appears to indicate when the message reached the recipient. However, concluding this without an experiment is hard, so that tag is ignored for now.
- The actual message is enclosed in <msg> tags.
- Usernames are not present; however, the direction of the message is included. In this case, you can look to other logs belonging to jitsi and conclude that the username of the local user is "mille". This particular log file is named "DDDUDE", indicating that the remote user is named "DDDUDE".

Having identified the information that is needed from the chat log, it is now possible to manually format the chat log. A more feasible option is to create a script that automatically does the job. For this example, a script was created using Powershell. For the sake of this example, the script fetches the information and presents it in a CSV-file, as displayed in Fig. 8.10. Finaly, the <msg> content was stripped so that it only included the message in plain text. The stripping was done using search and replace in a common text editor. The script is present in Chap. 14.

Sender	Message	Timestamp
DDDUDE	zup_	2017-06-27T13:16:07.826+0200
mille	kollar lite affÃ¤rer....sj?	2017-06-27T13:16:21.179+0200
DDDUDE	samma, lurar p[vad som ar vart att sa	2017-06-27T13:16:42.293+0200
mille	hur sÃ¤krar du?	2017-06-27T13:16:52.792+0200
DDDUDE	kor engelsk dator, svart lista ut vart ja	2017-06-27T13:17:20.785+0200
mille	tror inte det funkar, ,lira tor!	2017-06-27T13:17:30.963+0200
DDDUDE	har kollat pa det, vet inte, krangligt!	2017-06-27T13:17:46.289+0200

Fig. 8.10 Formatted jitsi log

8.10 Analyzing Unorganized Data

A hard drive will usually contain data that is best described as unorganized. This will, for instance, include slack space. There are also other sources of information that can be treated as unorganized data during a forensic examination, with great result. These sources include Pagefile and memory dumps. The Hiberfile, created when Windows is put into hibernation, can also be treated as unorganized data. Note that Pagefile, Hiberfile, and memory dumps are not really unorganized and can be analyzed in a more structured manner. An introduction to memory analysis is given in Chap. 11. Anyhow, common for these data sources is that they are not handled as the rest of the operating system, making them a source of artifacts that can be extremely good!

Pagefile and Hiberfile will usually contain the same type of information as a memory dump. The Pagefile is used by the computer when it needs to swap parts of the working memory and dump them somewhere else. The Hiberfile saves the current machine state when a Windows computer is put into hibernation and is used to enable the computer to wake up again. The information found here can commonly be very useful as it usually includes what the computer has been working within a very near past; this is especially true for the memory dumps. Further, when a computer is viewing encrypted material or reading e-mail and likewise, this information is stored in a decrypted state in memory, and thus this type of information can be recovered from memory, Pagefile or Hiberfile.

As for the slack space, it usually contains traces of data that used to reside on the computer. Consider a case where a file that fills up five clusters is deleted and a new file that is four and a half cluster large takes its place. The new file will not yet have overwritten the last half cluster, which is considered file slack. The nature of slack tells us that it can contain fragments of any type of file and therefore include any sort of information.

Treating data as unorganized implies that you have no idea what to expect in term of file structures, metadata, and likewise. Thus, we are left with raw searches as our means of analysis. You should know that the data sources discussed in this section are commonly quite large and doing raw searches over large datasets can be time-consuming. However, the nature of these data sources makes it possible to find extremely useful information and the effort is therefore often worthwhile. In my own experience, key evidence has been found using raw searches in especially memory dumps and Pagefile at several occasions. At one time, I was able to recover several decrypted versions of several encrypted e-mails from a web based e-mail service. The e-mails recovered could tie the suspect to an alias used to sell a lot of drugs online and landed the suspect several years of jail time.

Well then, analyzing unorganized data comes down to two things: searching and making something of the results. Searching is usually done using keywords and using regular expressions that are used to search for patterns. Depending on what you are looking for you will have to figure out appropriate search terms. A tip is to collect search terms that were successful so that you do not need to reinvent the search terms every time. One way to figure out search terms is to analyze raw data of information that is similar to the information you are looking for. That is, if you are looking for e-mail, you should analyze how e-mails are usually stored on disk and create your search terms based on that analysis. You could also include terms related to the case you are working on in your searches.

At this point, I want to stress the usefulness of building regular expressions to search for patterns instead of just using precise keywords. Regular expressions allow you to do searches for patterns, such as telephone numbers, e-mail addresses, or credit card numbers and to include several spellings of a term in one search word. For instance, we all know that an e-mail address is made up from some signs, followed by a "@" followed by some signs, a dot and top domain. Using regular expressions, as implemented by FTK, we can express an e-mail address as follows (Note that a perfect expression would have to be much longer): [A-Za-z0-9]+@ [A-Za-z0-9]+\. [A-Za-z]{2}.

The first brackets tell the expression to look for any of the letters a–z or numbers 0–9, then the + says that this can be repeated one or more times. The next part of the expression is a "@" stating that the next part of the pattern is an "@". Then, we have a series of a–z and 0–9 again followed by a dot. The dot in regular expressions means "any character" but in this case a backslash is put in front of the dot. A backslash in front of a symbol that has a meaning forces the regular expression to interpret the symbol literary. The final bracket is used to match top domains; therefore, the brackets say to look for the letters a–z. The "2" in the curly brackets states that the letter should be repeated twice. Searching for this regular expression would include all e-mail addresses that are complete matches to the expression.

After doing a search, you need to interpret the results. A common way to interpret results of a search in unorganized data is to look at the data surrounding the search hit. Consider the following example of when the term "wild-man" was used to search in a memory dump. One of the hits and surrounding data is presented in Fig. 8.11.

Looking at the data, you can see that the hit is from the string "username is wild-man". Adjacent to the string, you can see the data "New Text document.txt"

```
················FILE0···k-··········8···h···················;%··2·············`···
········H·······A·ç·OïÒ·1·ø·OïÒ·1·ø·OïÒ·A·ç·OïÒ·  ·························
@4.v····0··p············T······%······A·ç·OïÒ·A·ç·OïÒ·A·ç·OïÒ·A·ç·OïÒ·········
········ ·······|·f·i·l·e·3·.·t·x·t····@···(·················óÿ,··Tç··Ï·PV°éÎ
···0···················username is wild-man····ÿÿÿÿ·yG···N·e·w··T·e·x·t··D·o·
c·u·m·e·n·t·.·t·x·t···························ÿÿÿÿ·yG···················
·······································································
```

Fig. 8.11 Result after a keyword search

and "file3.txt". This could be interpreted as a trace of a text file containing the information "username is wild-man". Another conclusion could be that the text file was likely named file3.txt.

Analyzing unorganized data is like many other things in digital forensics, about understanding how the data you are looking for may be represented and being able to interpret data that seems unstructured and sometimes strange. It should also be stressed that being successful in this kind of searches is to a large extent down to experience—knowing what you look for and what you can usually found. That being said, unorganized data sources are a great source of evidence that should not be overlooked.

8.11 Questions and Tasks

Here are the questions for this chapter.

1. What is the install date of the computer you are working on?
2. What is the name of the time zone your computer is configured to use and when is the computer set to adjust time for daylight savings?
3. What is the username and RID of the default administrators account on your computer?
4. What is the starting sector and size, in gigabytes, of your system partition?
5. A file deleted from a computer can often be recovered with ease, explain why?
6. What is needed to make the content of a ZIP-archive part of an index?
7. What is Exif data and why is it relevant in digital forensics?
8. If you are asked to look for hidden partitions in unallocated space, what would you do?

References

AccessData. (2013). *AccessData forensics*. AccessData group.
EaseUS. (2017). EaseUs partition recovery wizard. Available online: https://www.easeus.com/partition-recovery/ [Fetched: 2017-07-01].
Guidance Software. (2016). *EnCase computer forensics II*. Guidance Software.
Knutsson, T. (2016). *Filesystem Timestamps: What Makes Them Tick?* SANS Institute

Rusbarsky, K. L. (2012). A forensic comparison of NTFS and FAT32 file systems. Available online: http://www.marshall.edu/forensics/files/RusbarskyKelsey_Research-Paper-Summer-2012.pdf [Fetched: 2017-07-06].

SoftXpantion. (2009). Metadata in Microsoft Office and in PDF documents. Available online: https://www.soft-xpansion.eu/files/cc/Metadata.pdf [Fetched: 2017-07-06].

Zacker, C. (2014). *Installing and configuring Windows Server 2012 R2*. Wiley.

Chapter 9
Some Common Questions

Abstract In some cases, a forensic examination is just about finding a picture, text or e-mail. However, it is very common that the forensic expert is tasked with answering more complex questions such as determining who the user of a computer is or if a computer was remote controlled. While providing a definite answer to such a question is often almost impossible, this chapter introduces three methods that can be used to tackle those requests. First, analysis of applications is an attempt to complete a deep examination of applications related to a specific task, for instance, remote controlling computers. The idea is that analyzing the computer for any trace of such software could provide an indication of whether it existed or not. The next method is scenario testing where the forensic expert tries to find evidence that favors, or disproves a stated scenario. The final method, useful for tying a person to some action, is Timelining where the forensic expert tries to cross-reference criminal actions with actions that can identify the computer user.

Keywords Application analysis · Timelining · Forensic analysis

The aim of this chapter is to discuss some questions that are common for a computer forensic examiner to be tasked with. The intent is not to provide a precise guideline that will work every time. Rather, this chapter presents an approach that can be used to tackle the questions. The answers are based on the authors own experience of answering these questions and defending the conclusions in court. Note that you can roughly categorize questions as "yes/no" or exploratory questions. Questions that can be answered yes or no are quite troublesome. The reason is that you may find what you are looking for and answer yes. However, not finding what you are looking does not really mean that you should answer no. Consider a case where you are asked if a picture was ever present on a cell phone. Finding the picture or traces of it would defiantly be a strong yes. However, not finding the picture doesn't mean that the picture was never on the phone, it doesn't even mean that it isn't on the phone right now. As such, answering such a question with a strong no is plain wrong. A better answer would be that the picture could not be

© The Author(s) 2017

J. Kävrestad, *Guide to Digital Forensics*, SpringerBriefs in Computer Science,
https://doi.org/10.1007/978-3-319-67450-6_9

found during the examination. You may stretch to make the conclusion that it indicates that the picture was never present on the phone.

9.1   Was the Computer Remote Controlled?

When you are able to present evidence found on a suspect's computer, a common objection is that the computer must have been remote controlled leading to a need for examining if the computer was remote controlled or not. This is a perfect example of a "yes/no" question where answering no is troublesome. However, based on the author's experience there are three good approaches on how to answer this question, namely;

- Analysis of applications
- Scenario testing
- Timelining.

Application analysis and Scenario testing will be described in the rest of this section. Timelining is good for determining the user of the computer and will be described in the next section.

9.1.1   Analysis of Applications

Analysis of applications is an approach that attempts to look for all possible evidences of remote control software or malware and if any is encountered, analyze that software. The aim is to analyze if the computer contains any software that can be used to remote controlling the computer. This is an approach that is quite troublesome for several reasons including;

- It is common for a computer to contain remote controlling software, making it very troublesome to report a no and defend that in court.
- The best possible result is that the computer doesn't contain any remote controlling software at the moment.

However, this approach is quite common and even if it is discouraged by the author a brief description seems necessary. To follow this approach you will need a fair bit of knowledge into what remote controlling software's that exist. Among the most common are:

- Remote desktop built into Windows, standard port number 3389
- Different implementations of VPN, protocol and port number depends on the application used
- Different implementations of SSH, standard port number 22
- TeamViewer, standard port number 5938.

An examination would include looking for those softwares among the softwares that are installed or, if possible, has been installed on the computer. This is done by looking into, for instance, the list of active processes, the "program" and "program files" folders and the "appdata" folder for each user. Since remote controlling software is communicating using port numbers that are not commonly open in the firewall, analysis of the firewall rules is also a part of this approach. If you find any remote controlling software among installed applications, the next step is to analyze the log files of the application to see if it has actually been used and how. If you find that the ports belonging to remote controlling applications are closed, this is further evidence in favor of the statement that the computer was not remote controlled. However, if you find that the ports are open, you are forced to report that the computer was likely remote controlled—or at least that it was possible to remote control the computer. To summarize, following this approach will lead, most likely, to one of the following results and conclusions:

- No traces of remote controlling software or open ports relating to remote controlling software leading to the conclusion that the computer does not currently contain remote controlling software indicating that it has not been remote controlled.
- Traces of remote controlling software exist but analysis of those applications reveal that they were never used leading to the conclusion that the computer does not currently contain remote controlling software indicating that it has not been remote controlled.
- No traces of remote controlling software exist but open ports relating to remote controlling software was found leading to an inconclusive conclusions since it's not possible to tell why the ports are open.
- Traces of remote controlling software exist and analysis of those applications reveal that they were used leading to the conclusion that the computer has been remote controlled.

When following this approach it is also essential to exclude malware as a source of remote controlling. To do this, it is suggested to search the computer for malware using at least two different antivirus programs. Any malware found should be further analyzed to exclude them as sources of remote control.

9.1.2 Scenario Testing

Another approach is to test if a scenario is possible or not. While this method is easier to use it does require that it is possible to establish a scenario for testing. To establish a scenario, the suspect pleading that his computers were remote controlled should be asked how. The suspect often answers with a scenario that can be tested. For instance, the suspect may say that the evidence is the result of malware or that Windows remote desktop is enabled and must have been used. Given this information, you can, instead of scanning for all possible traces of remote controlling software, analyze if the suspects claim holds true.

For instance, if the suspect does indeed state that Windows remote desktop is enabled on his computer and may even say that he has seen the mouse move around from time to time, then you should investigate Windows remote desktop. To begin, remote desktop requires that there are rules added to the Windows firewall to allow remote desktop connections. Also, remote desktop has to be configured to allow incoming connections. If those settings are not present, that is a sign that the suspect's statement is false. Moreover, you can often find log entries in event viewer that shows if anyone logged on to the computer using remote desktop. The best way to analyze Windows log files is to extract the log files from the image you are examining and analyze them in Windows event viewer. In this case, the log entry would be found in the Security log located at the path: C:\Windows\System32 \winevt\Logs\Security.evtx.

Each type of event has a unique event ID and the event ID for remote desktop logons are "4624." Searching for the event ID will return any log entries related to logins over remote desktop, an example of such entry is provided in Fig. 9.1.

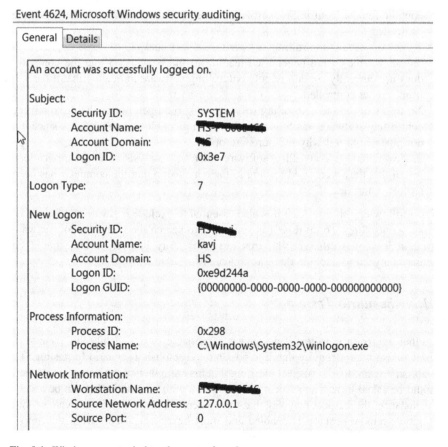

Fig. 9.1 Windows remote desktop log entry from logon

Finding log entries, enabled remote desktop or firewall rules will render you unable to disprove the suspects claim. However, if neither is present, that is a strong sign that the suspects claim is wrong. Not only will that disprove that the computer was remote controlled, it may also help diminish the suspect's credibility.

9.2   Who Was Using the Computer?

While an investigation, criminal or corporate, is interested in finding out who did something, computer forensics is commonly limited to describing what a computer was doing. Deciding who was behind the keyboard is sometimes seen as impossible and even if it is not impossible it is surely a difficult task. The troubles that arise are that it is indeed impossible to tell the identity of the users that made the computer commit a certain action. The discussion on remote controlling software and the possibility of several persons having access to the same computer testifies to that.

While it is impossible (and infeasible) to determine the identity of the person using the computer in general, it can be possible to determine the computer user, with some certainty, at specific times. For instance, analyzing chat logs, online banking logins and other pieces of information can tell you who used the computer at a certain time. Also, in a default Windows environment, it is only possible for one graphical session at the time bringing the fact that if you can identify one user you can also be quite sure that she is the only user at that precise time. This knowledge allows us to attempt to determine the identity of a user using Timelining.

Timelining is an approach where you attempt to make it unreasonable to believe that someone else than a specific person committed actions, usually a crime, using the computer that is target for examination. The idea with Timelining is that you find events relating to criminal activity and plot them on a time line. You then look for artifacts that identify the user of the computer and plots those events on the same time line. Identifying events can include filling out forms online, chat messages, online banking logins, and social media events. What you are looking for is overlaps between criminal and identifying events, or at least events in close proximity to each other. Consider the sample timeline in Fig. 9.2.

As you can see in the sample time line, the computer was used at three periods during a 12 h period. Some action related to frauds are committed at each period and overlapping with events where the user is presenting himself as Joakim Kävrestad. While you can never neglect the possibility that the criminal is posing as someone to obfuscate an investigation, a time line like this does indicate that the person committing the fraudulent activities is indeed Joakim Kävrestad. The more overlaps you can identify and the longer the period containing the overlaps, the stronger indication of who the actual user is. However, make sure to fully understand the timestamps of the events you are using in your Timelining!

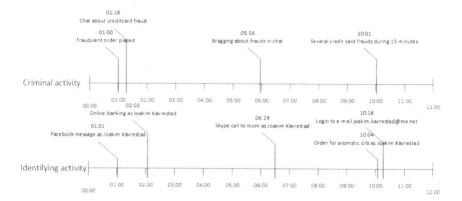

Fig. 9.2 Sample time line

9.3   Was This Device Ever at Site X?

So far we mostly discussed the evidence contained in a digital device but there are times when the physical location of a device is more interesting than the data in it. This can, for instance, be the case in investigations of murder, rape, assault, and likewise. If a suspect claims that he was never on the scene of the crime it can be possible to prove or disprove that statement.

Analyzing where a device has been can basically be done by analyzing two types of artifacts, GPS coordinates and network connections. GPS coordinates are put onto many different types of events. Depending on the device settings GPS information can for instance be included in photos, Facebook activity, and tweets. Thus, if someone is committing a crime and takes a photo, updates Facebook or sends a tweet during or in close proximity to the crime, it can be possible to position the device, and thus providing an indication of the suspect's position. In FTK, it is possible to do a meta carve, as previously discussed, to uncover GPS coordinated in file metadata. You could also use a regular expression to do a live search for GPS coordinates. Since it is common for activity in web browsers to end up in some unorganized data, a search is suggested. The search will also cover GPD coordinated found in files.

Another way to go is to analyze if the device has been connected to any network close to the crime scene. Depending on the type of device, this information is located in different places. However, a good suggestion is to collect information about wireless networks close to the crime scene and then use the network names as search terms. A drawback of looking for connections instead of GPS coordinates is that the connection information is seldom timestamped meaning that your best conclusion will often be that device was at the crime scene at some time. GPS coordinates are commonly found in data that also contains a timestamp, this information enables you to say that the device was at a particular site at a particular time.

9.4   Questions and Tasks

The task for this chapter is for you to examine your own computer in an attempt to prove that you are the user of your computer and that your computer has been at your home.

Chapter 10
FTK Specifics

Abstract This chapter provides the reader with an overview of the functions of AccessData FTK and registry viewer. The aim of the chapter is to provide a student with the fundamentals of the software so that she can start working with the products without being totally in the dark about how they work. The chapter begins with describing the process of creating a case and configuring preprocessing options in FTK. Then, the chapter provides an orientation of the most commonly used functions in FTK. While the orientation does not cover all functions in FTK, it does provide enough knowledge to let the reader efficiently learn FTK on her own. After exploring FTK, the chapter describes the basic functions of AccessData Registry viewer. Registry viewer is a tool that is used to analyze Windows registry hives. Registry viewer contains functionality such as advanced searching and reporting functionality and interprets several types of registry data automatically.

Keywords Preprocessing · FTK · Registry viewer

This is a chapter that is 100% devoted to describing how to use AccessData FTK and AccessData Registry viewer. It is intentionally placed in the end, but those of you who are FTK users could benefit from reading it at the beginning of the practical section. As most software vendors do, AccessData submits user manuals with their product and while this book does not intend to provide a complete user manual, the aim of this chapter is to provide enough knowledge about the covered products to enable you to get a smooth start on your forensic experience. In addition to overviews of FTK and Registry viewer, an overview of PRTF was presented in Chap. 7 and FTK imager was presented in Chap. 6. Since this chapter does not introduce any new forensic knowledge, there are no questions or tasks in the end of this chapter.

© The Author(s) 2017

J. Kävrestad, *Guide to Digital Forensics*, SpringerBriefs in Computer Science,
https://doi.org/10.1007/978-3-319-67450-6_10

10.1 FTK: Create a Case

When you installed FTK and logged on to your instance of FTK for the very first time you are basically faced with a database interface that is empty. The interface is presented in Fig. 10.1.

Starting with the top menu bar, the different menus have the following uses:

- File: No other use than to close FTK.
- Database: Tasks related to managing users of the database and configuration of the actual database.
- Case: Tasks related to specific cases, this section will end with a description of those.
- Tools: Tasks related to configuring FTK, for instance, if you want to use distributed case processing.
- Manage: In this menu, you can edit different tasks related to case analysis, for instance, you can manage and create a signature for data carving.
- Help: One would think that this menu contains a help section or user manual, but it only contains some licensing information.

Next, the cases pane will list the cases in your database and the right pane will show you information about the marked case. To create a new case, hit the case menu and select New. This will take you to the dialog shown in Fig. 10.2.

The first two parts are the case name and description. Input whatever is enforced by your organization, or otherwise reasonable. The next part is the Case Folder, this is where your case will be stored. Next, select where the database related to the case will be stored; it is common to store it in the case folder. Note that the case database and amount of case data can be rather large and be intensively used by FTK. It is, therefore, a good idea to have a dedicated hard drive or storage server for FTK cases. Before you hit OK to create the case you need to decide on, and possibly

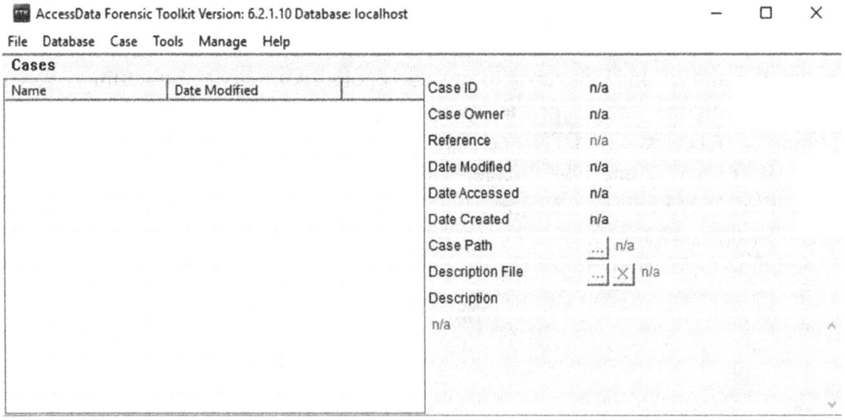

Fig. 10.1 FTK database interface

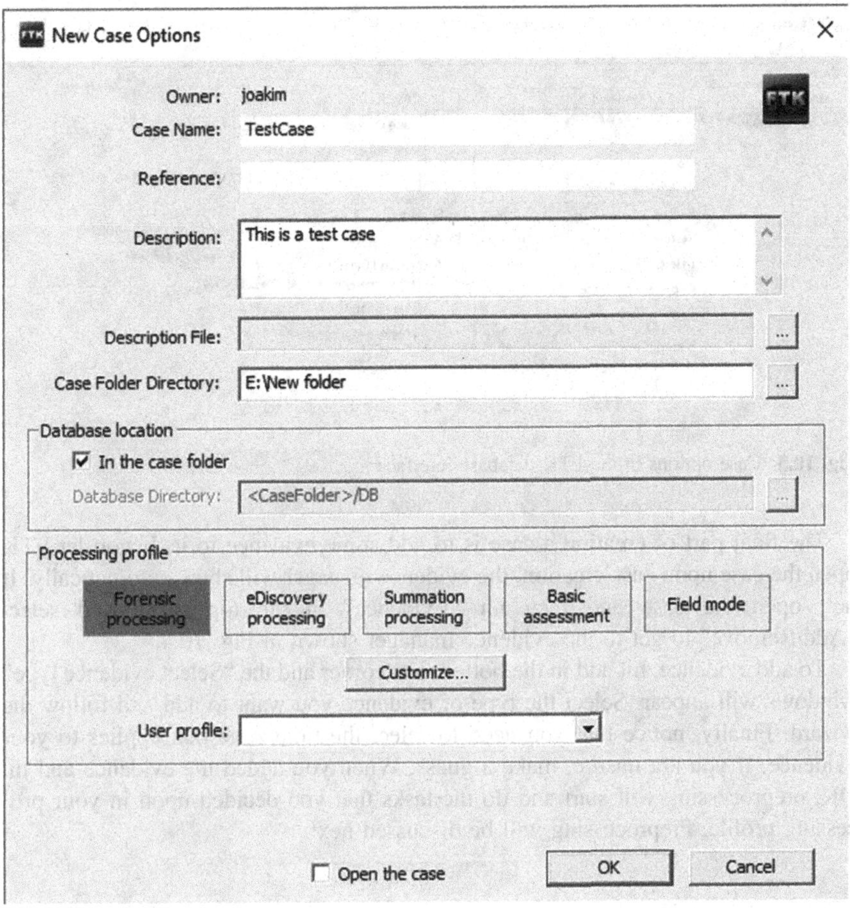

Fig. 10.2 Add a new case

modify a processing profile. To modify or review the processing profile, hit Customize. This will be your preprocessing settings, depicting the processes that will be done to every piece of evidence you add to the case. Preprocessing is discussed in greater detail in the next section.

Upon hitting OK, FTK will as default open the case and prompt you to add some evidence. In this case, the "Open the case" checkbox was checked out so that the case could be reviewed in the database interface. As seen in Fig. 10.3, the newly created case appeared in the case list. Also, some information about the case is listed in the right pane. From this interface, it is possible to backup and restore cases. Note the two types of backup; Backup and archive. Backup is meant to be used for backups during the lifetime of the case and archive is used to archive the case for storing after it is completed. Archive and detach will create a case archive and remove the case from the case list, and thus the database.

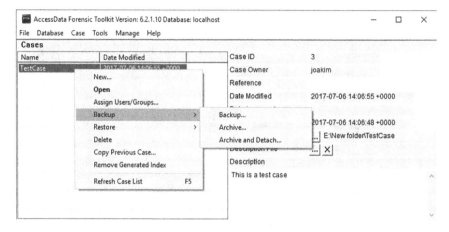

Fig. 10.3 Case options in the FTK database interface

The final part of creating a case is to add some evidence to it. If you let FTK open the case upon case creation, the evidence manager will show automatically. If not, open the case and then hit "Evidence" in the top menu and select "Add/Remove" to get to the evidence manager shown in Fig. 10.4.

To add evidence, hit add in the bottom left corner and the "Select evidence type" windows will appear. Select the type of evidence you want to add and follow the wizard. Finally, notice that you need to select the time zone that applies to your evidence. If you are unsure, make a guess. When you added the evidence and hit OK, preprocessing will start and do the tasks that you decided upon in your processing profile. Preprocessing will be discussed next.

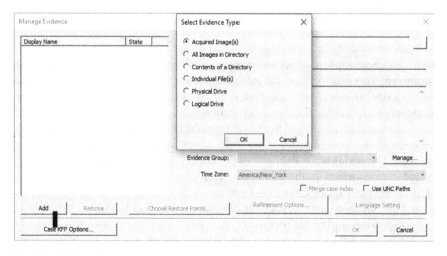

Fig. 10.4 FTK evidence manager

10.2 FTK: Preprocessing

As seen during case creation, there are some preprocessing profiles that were already created. If you want to review or modify a profile you can hit customize, that will bring you to the menu shown in Fig. 10.5 (you can get to the same menu by hitting Refinement options from the evidence manager).

The top options concerns hashing and automatic file detection. Since two identical files will have the same hash value, hashing can be used to identify duplicate files. To generate file hashes, check the boxes that correspond to the hash algorithms you want to use. *Flag duplicate files* are used to, well, flag duplicate files based on an evaluation of hash values. *KFF* (Known File Filter) can be described as

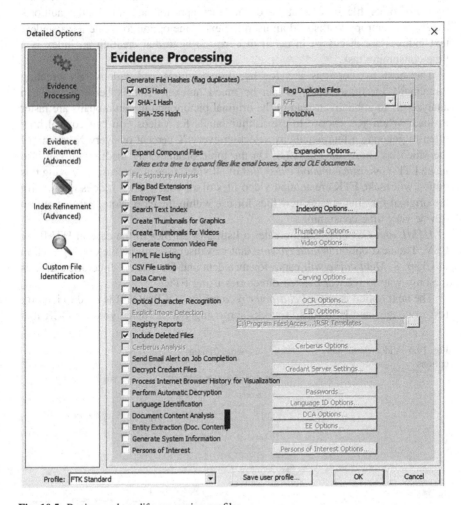

Fig. 10.5 Review and modify processing profiles

an add-on that has to be installed separately. KFF allows you to use a list containing hashes of known files, such as installers, Windows files, and other files that are seldom of interest. FTK will evaluate all files in the case against the hashes in KFF and flag those that are included in KFF. The advantage here is that you do not need to spend time analyzing uninteresting files. The last option in the top box is *Photo DNA* that can be used to identify identical or similar pictures.

Expand compound files is used to expand compound files, as discussed in Chap. 8. *File signature Analysis* is a function that looks at file signatures and file's extensions, and flags all files where the file signature and file extension does not match. This allows you to identify files where the file type has been changed, possibly indicating an attempt to hide information.

Entropy test is a function that attempts to evaluate the randomness of the data in different files. The idea is to be able to identify encrypted data. However, there are so many other file types that have data that appears random. In the author's experience, entropy test is seldom useful. Next is the option to create a text index, text indexes are discussed in detail in Chap. 7. Note that creating an index is a time-consuming task.

The next two options are for handling pictures and videos. By creating thumbnails for those, analysis can be much quicker. This is because you can analyze the thumbnails instead of the original picture and the thumbnails are faster to load. When you choose to create thumbnails for videos you can control how often to generate a thumbnails by selecting every X percent or every X second of the video, as shown in Fig. 10.6. On the topic of analyzing media, you can also make FTK *Generate common video files* of all video files in you case. Selecting this option will make FTK create mp4 video files of all your videos, it does not modify the original files but creates new files for use within the case. Note that this option can be very time-consuming.

HTML and CSV file listing creates a listing of all files in the case in HTML or CSV. The next option is *data carving* that was discussed in the file carving section of Chap. 8. *Meta carve* will carve for metadata and for deleted directories. This is the only way to recover deleted directories using FTK.

The next option is *optical character recognition* (OCR). OCR is used to identify text in images and PDF files, it works surprisingly well. When you use OCR it is

Fig. 10.6 Video thumbnail options

Video Thumbnail Options   ✕

┌─Thumbnail Generation Frequency ─────────────────────────┐
│ ⦿ Percent   │
│   │5│   ⬍ (1 thumbnail every "n"% of the video)   │
│ ○ Interval   │
│   │600│ ⬍ (1 thumbnail every "n" seconds)   │
└──┘

                                      │   OK   │   │ Cancel │

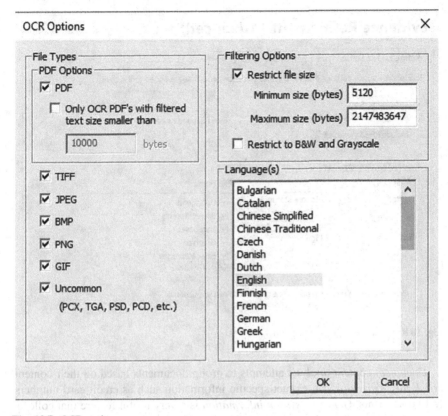

Fig. 10.7 OCR options

possible to search for text content in pictures and add text from pictures to the case index. The options you can use for OCR can be seen in Fig. 10.7. In short, you can select what file types to apply OCR to and choose to exclude files based on size. Note that OCR is a very time-consuming task.

Explicit Image detection is an add-on that can be used to identify explicit images, such as child exploitation. Next, the *registry report* option can be used to automatically create reports on registry data based on templates and *include deleted files* is used to make FTK consider deleted files for all processing options.

Cerberus analysis is another add-on, this one is used for malware analysis. Next, you can make FTK send an e-mail when a job is complete and *decrypt credant files*. In the author's experience, encryption using credant is not common.

Process internet browser history for visualization is an option that will process browsing history so that you can view the history in a timeline. *Perform automatic decryption* is not as magical as it sounds, but can be used to automatically decrypt several encrypted file types. It does, however, require you to submit the password. *Language identification* will make FTK analyze the beginning of each document in an attempt to identify the language in which it is written.

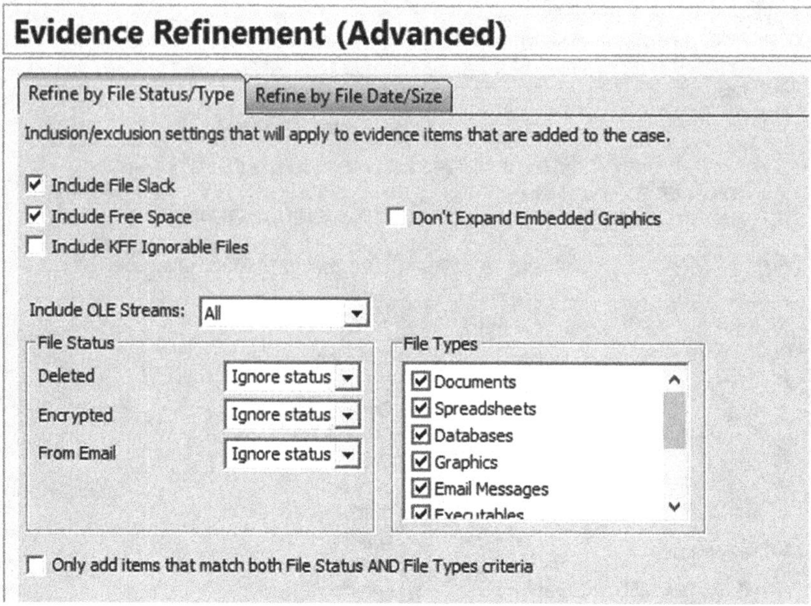

Fig. 10.8 Evidence refinement option

Document content analysis attempts to group documents based on their content and *Entity extraction* can extract specific information such as credit card numbers from documents. *Generate system information* is a very useful feature that collects system information such as owner information, users on the system and more. Finally, the *Persons of interest* is a feature designed to show connections between phone and e-mail evidence in a case.

As a final touch, you can limit what files that are added to the case and considered for the index by Index and Case refinement in the right pane. This can be useful if you have a search warrant that is limited to some files or to a certain time span, or want to analyze specific files for some other reason. The evidence refinement options are seen in Fig. 10.8.

10.3   FTK: Overview

The final part of the FTK introduction is an overview of the actual FTK interface. This overview shows some of the views and features of FTK but is in no way exhaustive. The idea is to present some of the more common areas and some less obvious but good features. An overview of the interface is presented in Fig. 10.9, the different panes and menus are denoted in the picture.

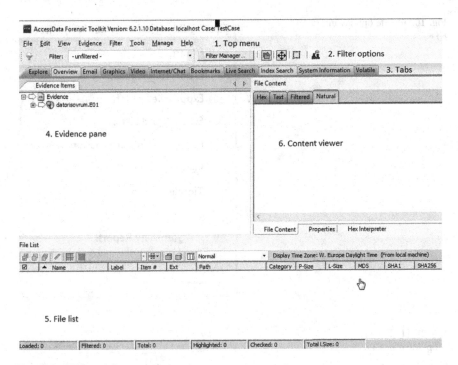

Fig. 10.9 FTK overview

Looking at the top menu, some of the drop-downs deserves to be mentioned. First, the File drop-down is where you find some good features including options to export system information and a word list. The word list is based on your index and can be imported into PRTK. The file drop-down is shown in Fig. 10.10.

The Edit and View drop-downs are quite self-explaining and best discovered by testing, leading to the important evidence menu. The evidence drop-down is where you can reach the evidence manager, by pressing "Add/remove". If you notice that the processes you ran during preprocessing were not enough you can run more processing by hitting additional analysis. You can also use the evidence drop-down to import a memory dump into FTK. The evidence drop-down in presented in Fig. 10.11.

The final drop-down that is highlighted in this chapter is manage. The manage drop-down contains options that can be used to change settings related to KFF and PhotoDNA as well as a means of configuring your own file carvers. However, perhaps the most usable options available in the manage drop-down is the Filter and Column managers. Using filters in FTK you can decide on what content you want to show. For instance, if you are only looking for pictures you can apply a filter that makes FTK only display pictures. Likewise, you can filter on file creation date, file size, and several other parameters.

Fig. 10.10 File options in
FTK

Fig. 10.11 Evidence
drop-down in FTK

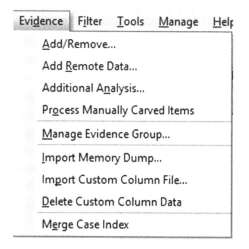

The column manager is used to control what columns to display in the file list. There are columns available for many different types of data and controlling what columns that you display enables you to control what data you want to see in the file list. The manage drop-down is shown in Fig. 10.12.

Moving on from the top menu, the next part of the FTK interface that deserves attention is the filter options. To begin, the filter option contains a drop-down of all filters that you may apply to your case. When you apply a filter, only files that meet the criteria stated by the filter will be displayed by FTK. To indicate that a filter is active, the File list gets a yellowish background. As a tip from the real world, if you

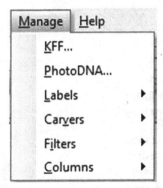

Fig. 10.12 Manage drop-down

are examining some folder and files seem to be missing, it is likely that you forgot to turn filtering off. You can turn filtering off by hitting the icon that looks like a funnel, at the far left of the filter options. As is displayed in Fig. 10.13, FTK comes with a bunch of pre-created filters that you can use, but you can also create your own filters in the filter manager that you access by hitting Filter Manager.

Next, there is the evidence pane. The evidence pane shows the evidence items you included in your case as a browsable tree structure. Marking a folder in the evidence pane will make FTK list the content of that folder in the file list. A very useful function in the evidence pane is "Quick picks". "Quick picks" is a function that lets you choose a folder and FTK will display the content of that folder and all of its subfolders in the file list. You can enable "Quick picks" for several folders at once. Note that marking a folder in the evidence pane will have no effect when "Quick picks" is active. The evidence pane is displayed in Fig. 10.14. Enable "Quick picks" for a folder by hitting the arrow in front of the folder.

Note the options [root] and [orphan] under the file system for Partition 2. [root] denotes the root of the file system and [orphan] lists orphan files. Orphan files are files that do not appear to have a parent folder.

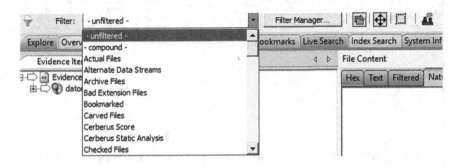

Fig. 10.13 Filter options in FTK

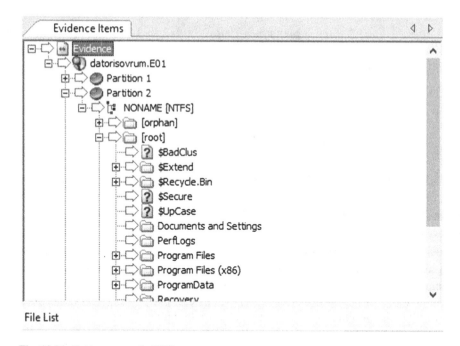

Fig. 10.14 Evidence pane in FTK

Next part to discuss is the file list where the contents of folders selected in the evidence pane are displayed. As a default, file name, path, time stamps, and some more data are shown in the different columns, as shown in Fig. 10.15.

Before each item in the list there is a checkbox. You can check files as a means of selecting files that you want to perform a certain action too, such as searching or

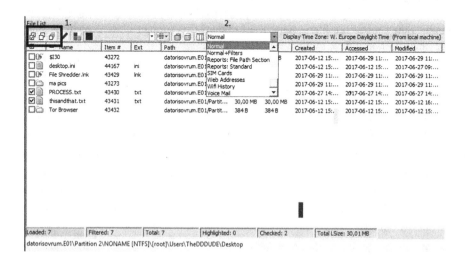

Fig. 10.15 FTK file listing

bookmarking. The bottom of the file list shows you some statistics such as how many checked files there are in your case, how many files that are currently in the file list, etc. Note that the only way to uncheck a file is to do it manually or by pressing the "uncheck all" button. The "uncheck all" button is the rightmost bottom in the square marked 1. in Fig. 10.15. The middle button is used to uncheck any checked items in the current file list and the leftmost button will check all currently listed items. For each file, information such as name, path, size, and timestamps is shown as the default FTK behavior. You can control what information that is displayed by changing column settings, in the drop-down denoted by 2.

When you mark a file in the file list it will be displayed in the content viewer, as shown in Fig. 10.16. The bar above the content viewer decides how to view the file data. The natural view tries to display the file as it is intended to be viewed. A picture as a picture, a word document as a word document and so on. FTK can view a large number of different file types. The filtered view displays the file as ASCII data but excludes the data that FTK does not deem as interesting. The text view shows the file as plain text if applicable and finally the hex view shows the file data in hexadecimal and ASCII.

The bar below the viewer decides what to show, file content will show the actual file and Properties will show the file metadata. Finally, the hex interpreter will try to interpret and report certain hexadecimal values that may be present in the viewed file.

One of the most wonderful functions of FTK is that it groups all files in a case by category. By going to the overview tab, you can browse the data in the case by file category or file extension instead of looking through the folder structure. If you know that you are looking for a document but have no clue about its whereabouts, the overview tab can be a great help. The overview tab is demonstrated in

Fig. 10.16 FTK content viewer

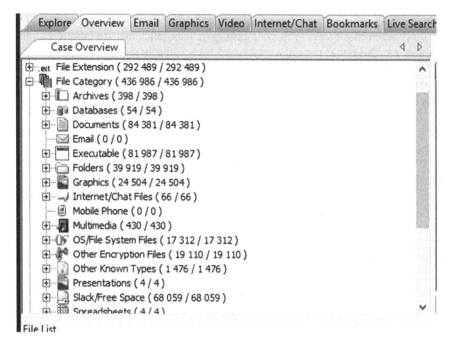

Fig. 10.17 Overview tab

Fig. 10.17. The rest of the tabs have quite self-explaining names. Explore them on your own!

The final thing presented about FTK in this book is what you can do to a file. Naturally, when you find a file you need to do something to it. To apply some action to a file in FTK. Simply right-click it and you will be presented with the options displayed in Fig. 10.18. Figure 10.18 also shows an example of "Quick picks" in action. In the picture, "Quick picks" was applied to the "Desktop" folder. Note the yellow mark on the parent folder, THEDDDUDE, which denotes that "quick pics" was applied to a sub-folder. Well then, highlighting some of the options available when you right-click a file, the options begin with Open, that opens the file in the default viewer for that file type in Windows. Using Open With you can open it in Windows using some other application. Next is the option to bookmark the file. You can add the file to an existing bookmark or create a new bookmark. The bookmarked files will appear under the Bookmarks tab.

The next option of interest is Visualize browser history that you can click if you selected to complete the appropriate process, as previously discussed. Then, you may export the file or export the file to an image. Exporting files to an image is useful when you are to send some files to someone else for further analysis. That concludes the introduction to FTK, hopefully, you have now seen enough to enable you to start working with FTK on your own.

Fig. 10.18 FTK file options

10.4 Registry Viewer: Overview

This section presents and overviews Registry viewer that is used to analyze registry hives. Working with Registry viewer you can analyze one hive at the time and if you need to extract data you would do that in a report. The main benefit of using Registry viewer over regedit is, in the author's opinion, better search utilities and that registry viewer interprets values that are written in formats that are hard to understand. Well, let's get at it by examining the registry viewer interface presented in Fig. 10.19.

Starting from the top, there is a top menu and then a menu with buttons, the important parts of those sections will be discussed next. The top left pane shows the registry hive you are currently examining as a browsable tree structure. The right view shows keys and their values and the bottom left pane shows properties

Fig. 10.19 Registry viewer overview

for the key you are currently working on. Next, have a closer look at the buttons in the button menu. The button menu in registry viewer provides a quick way to use the features that you will use most of the time. The button menu is displayed in Fig. 10.20.

Going from left to right, the purpose of each button is as follows:

- Open a registry hive in registry viewer; you can only analyze one hive at the time
- Get to full registry view, as opposed to common areas
- Enter report view to see what keys that are added to the report

Fig. 10.20 Button menu in registry viewer

- View common areas, pressing this button will make registry viewer show you the registry keys that are added to common areas. This function can be seen as a shortcut to information that is commonly of interest
- Generate report
- Add to report, used to add a key and its values to the report
- Add to report with children, used to add a key and its sub keys with corresponding values to the report
- Add to common areas, used to add a key to common areas for quick access in future examinations
- Remove from common areas
- View help.

While browsing the hive you are examining or using common areas are common ways to examine a registry hive there are times when you want to do a keyword search. A great way to do keyword searches is by advanced find, reachable by hitting edit in the top menu. Advanced find is displayed in Fig. 10.21.

As you can see in Fig. 10.21, this search function allows you to search for keywords present in keys or values and will display all search hits as a list. There is also a button that allows you to add search hits to the report. Our next topic of discussion is the properties pane, displayed in Fig. 10.22.

The example shows a case where a registry hive is analyzed using common areas. You can tell that a key is included in common areas by the key on the folder in the top left pane. In this case, the key "TimeZoneInformation" is examined. A summary of the data, in human readable format, is presented in the key properties

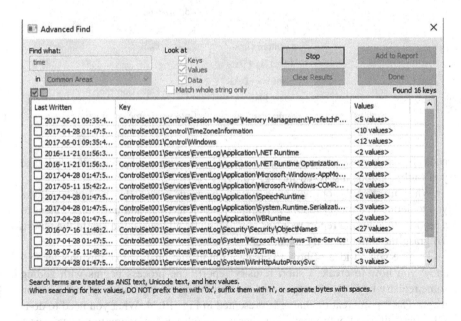

Fig. 10.21 Advanced find in registry viewer

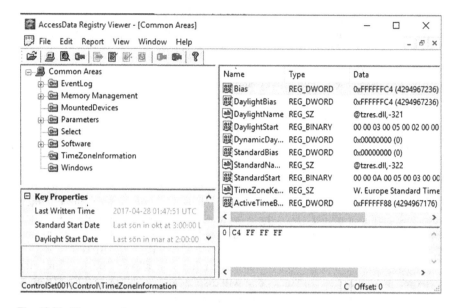

Fig. 10.22 Key properties

Fig. 10.23 Key options

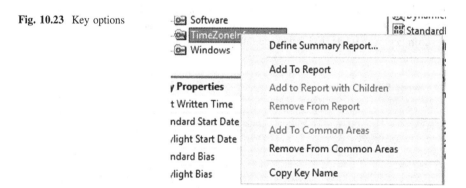

pane. To reach most actions you can do to a key you can right-click it, this will take you to the options displayed in Fig. 10.23.

While most of the options have already been discussed, the top option allows you to define a summary report. A summary report lets you add individual values to a report and a normal report requires you to include all values of a key to the report. To grasp the difference, try it yourself!

To give you an idea of how to create a report, the final part of this chapter will show you how to create a short registry report. The process begins with adding some registry key(s) to the report and starting the report generation from the button menu. The report creation dialog is presented in Fig. 10.24. What you need to do is selecting a title and output path. Another great option is the option to reduce excess

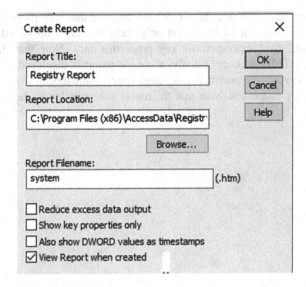

Fig. 10.24   Registry creation dialog

Registry Information

Registry Report

ControlSet001\Control\TimeZoneInformation

Last Written Time	2017-04-28 01:47:51 UTC
Standard Start Date	Last sön in okt at 3:00:00 Local
Daylight Start Date	Last sön in mar at 2:00:00 Local
Standard Bias	0
Daylight Bias	-60

Software

Last Written Time	2017-04-28 01:47:51 UTC

AccessData Registry Viewer

Fig. 10.25   Registry viewer report sample

output. This option will reduce how much information that is displayed in raw data format. You may also make the report only include what is displayed in the key properties pane, by checking show key properties only. Note that the report is created as an HTML package. Finally, a sample report is displayed in Fig. 10.25. This sample showed a report including time zone information using the option to only display key properties. Note that the report also includes the last written time for the registry hive.

Chapter 11
Basic Memory Analysis

Abstract Computer memory (RAM) is a great source of forensic artifacts as it
contains information that the computer worked on since the last reboot. Also,
information must take its true unencrypted form in memory, in order to be mean-
ingful for the user. From a forensic perspective, a memory dump can contain vital
information such as passwords, decrypted versions of encrypted data and malware
in its true form. This chapter provides the reader with an introduction to memory
analysis using the open source tool Volatility. Using Volatility rather than treating a
memory dump as a big blob of data allows the examiner to complete a more
structured analysis. This chapter demonstrates how to use Volatility to find several
key artifacts including list of user on the system, files loaded into memory and
information relating to Truecrypt, a tool used for encryption. The aim of the chapter
is to show the reader the basic functionality of Volatility so that the reader can
continue to learn memory analysis on his own.

Keywords Memory analysis · Volatility

Memory has, up until this point, been discussed as an unorganized data blob. This is
not really true, the memory does have a structure and can be analyzed in a structured way. While discussing the inner workings of storage in memory is well
beyond the scope of his book, some basics of memory analysis are presented in this
chapter. A very deep discussion on memory forensics using the tool Volatility is
given in the book "The art of memory forensics" by Ligh et al. (2014).

A very powerful tool that can be used for memory forensics, and is open source,
is Volatility (Volatility Foundation 2017). This section is devoted to providing an
introduction to using Volatility, note that all examples were created using a memory
dump from a computer running Windows XP. However, unless otherwise stated,
the examples should be accurate for newer versions of Windows as well. Volatility
is a command line tool that is available for Linux and Windows, a personal pref-
erence is to use is on Linux to get access to bash command line tools. The basic
syntax of Volatility is as follows:

```
Volatility –f memoryimage –profile=selectedmemoryprofile module
```

© The Author(s) 2017   117
J. Kävrestad, *Guide to Digital Forensics*, SpringerBriefs in Computer Science,
https://doi.org/10.1007/978-3-319-67450-6_11

```
analyzer@volabox:~/Desktop$ volatility -f testimg.vmem imageinfo
Volatility Foundation Volatility Framework 2.4
Determining profile based on KDBG search...

WARNING : volatility.obj        : Overlay structure tty_struct not present in vtypes
            Suggested Profile(s) : WinXPSP2x86, WinXPSP3x86 (Instantiated with WinXPSP2x86)
                      AS Layer1  : IA32PagedMemoryPae (Kernel AS)
                      AS Layer2  : FileAddressSpace (/home/analyzer/Desktop/testimg.vmem)
                      PAE type   : PAE
                           DTB   : 0x319000L
                          KDBG   : 0x80545b60
            Number of Processors : 1
       Image Type (Service Pack) : 3
               KPCR for CPU 0     : 0xffdff000
            KUSER_SHARED_DATA     : 0xffdf0000
            Image date and time  : 2011-01-06 14:50:19 UTC+0000
      Image local date and time  : 2011-01-06 09:50:19 -0500
analyzer@volabox:~/Desktop$ █
```

Fig. 11.1 Volatility imageinfo

Memoryimage is the path to the memory dump that you need to analyze. Different operating systems handle memory in different ways. Volatility uses so-called memory profiles to know what operating system and version the memory sample is from. Thus, selectedmemoryprofile is the memory profile you need Volatility to use. Finally, module is the task you want Volatility to run. Before you begin you need to figure out the memory profile to use. You can make Volatility analyze the memory sample using the *imageinfo* module, as shown in Fig. 11.1.

Looking to Fig. 11.1, you can see that Volatility suggests different profiles that can be used. Any will commonly work but otherwise it is a trial and error approach among the suggested profiles. Note that the profile name must be spelled with exact casing. *Imageinfo* will also report the time when the memory dump was created, expressed in UTC and local time. Starting of the memory analysis it can be a good idea to view processes that were active at the time that the memory dump was taken. Listing active processes will reveal what the computer was up to and provide insight into, for instance, if any encryption software or other software of interest for the investigation was running on the system. Listing processes is done with the *pslist* module, as demonstrated in Fig. 11.2.

```
analyzer@volabox:~/Desktop$ volatility -f testimg.vmem --profile="WinXPSP3x86" pslistVolatility Foundation Volatility
Framework 2.4
Offset(V)  Name                    PID   PPID  Thds   Hnds  Sess  Wow64 Start                    Exit
---------- --------------------- ------ ------ ------ ------ ----- ----- ------------------------ ------------
                                I
0x825c8830 System                  4      0    58     387  ------    0
0x823fe020 smss.exe               572      4     3      19  ------    0 2010-11-11 22:02:08 UTC+0000
0x82503220 csrss.exe             636    572    13     399     0      0 2010-11-11 22:02:13 UTC+0000
0x81f4c550 winlogon.exe          660    572    21     596     0      0 2010-11-11 22:02:14 UTC+0000
0x8207d5f0 services.exe          704    660    17     285     0      0 2010-11-11 22:02:15 UTC+0000
0x824264c0 lsass.exe             716    660    20     356     0      0 2010-11-11 22:02:15 UTC+0000
0x8230c5f8 vmacthlp.exe          872    704     2      26     0      0 2010-11-11 22:02:16 UTC+0000
0x8226cda0 svchost.exe       █   904    704    16     191     0      0 2010-11-11 22:02:16 UTC+0000
```

Fig. 11.2 Volatility pslist

```
analyzer@volabox:~/Desktop$ volatility -f testimg.vmem --profile="WinXPSP3x86" pstree
Volatility Foundation Volatility Framework 2.4
Name                                             Pid   PPid  Thds  Hnds Time
------------------------------------------------ ----- ----- ----- ---- ----
 0x825c8830:System                                  4     0    58   387 1970-01-01 00:00:00 UTC+0000
. 0x823fe020:smss.exe                             572     4     3    19 2010-11-11 22:02:08 UTC+0000
.. 0x81f4c550:winlogon.exe                        660   572    21   596 2010-11-11 22:02:14 UTC+0000
... 0x824264c0:lsass.exe                          716   660    20   356 2010-11-11 22:02:15 UTC+0000
... 0x8207d5f0:services.exe                       704   660    17   285 2010-11-11 22:02:15 UTC+0000
.... 0x823f2020:svchost.exe                       972   704     9   264 2010-11-11 22:02:17 UTC+0000
.... 0x824578b0:imapi.exe                        1040   704     5   114 2010-11-11 22:03:54 UTC+0000
.... 0x82284b80:vmtoolsd.exe                     1816   704     6   268 2010-11-11 22:02:30 UTC+0000
.... 0x82067858:svchost.ex                       1540   704     6    95 2010-11-11 22:02:26 UTC+0000
.... 0x822a0758:svchost.ex                       1068   704    58  1256 2010-11-11 22:02:17 UTC+0000
```

Fig. 11.3 Volatility pstree

```
analyzer@volabox:~/Desktop$ volatility -f testimg.vmem --profile="WinXPSP3x86" connscan
Volatility Foundation Volatility Framework 2.4
Offset(P)  Local Address            Remote Address            Pid
---------- ------------------------ ------------------------  ---
0x01eacc00 192.168.16.129:1039      65.55.185.26:443          1068
0x01fd3170 192.168.16.129:1040      207.46.21.58:80           1068
analyzer@volabox:~/Desktop$
```

Fig. 11.4 Volatility connscan

Each active process is listed and the process ID (PID) and process ID of the parent process (PPID) is reported. Using the module *pstree,* you can view the parent/child relationships in a more graphical manner. The output of *pstree* is shown in Fig. 11.3.

In some cases, it can be interesting to know the computers established network connections. This can grant you information about, malware, remote storage, running network services, and more. For Windows XP and previous, this information is viewed using the *connscan* module, as viewed in Fig. 11.4. For later versions of Windows, you can use *netscan* that produces similar results.

Some parts of the Windows registry are actually volatile and therefore lost when the computer reboots. For that reason, it can be interesting to analyze the registry hives loaded into memory. Using the *hivelist* module will tell you what registry hives that are loaded into memory. Since NTuser.dat for a user is loaded into memory when a user logs on to the system, listing the hives will also tell you what users that are or has been logged on to the system since the last system reboot. The output of the *hivelist* module is presented in Fig. 11.5.

When on the topic of registry data, you can use Volatility to examine userassist keys. Userassist keys are basically keys that get updated when a user does something and can, for instance, tell you what programs a user used. They can actually even tell you when a program was last used and how many times it has been used. Userassist keys are found using the *userassist* module, as shown in Fig. 11.6.

Looking at Fig. 11.6, it begins with listing a NTuser.dat file, in this case the one found in the administrator user folder. A time of last update is reported. This data should provide a rough idea on when the account was last used. The following is a list of items captured as userassist data. For instance, MSN.lnk that appears to be a shortcut (because of the lnk file extension) is listed. Count is reported as 14 telling

```
analyzer@volabox:~/Desktop$ volatility -f testimg.vmem --profile="WinXPSP3x86" hivelist
Volatility Foundation Volatility Framework 2.4
Virtual    Physical    Name
---------- ----------  ----
0x22ad700 0x198a4700 \Device\HarddiskVolume1\Documents and Settings\Administrator\Local Settings\Application Data\Mic
rosoft\Windows\UsrClass.dat
0x2239008 0x19413008 \Device\HarddiskVolume1\Documents and Settings\Administrator\NTUSER.DAT
0xe1bd85e0 0x0ec325e0 \Device\HarddiskVolume1\Documents and Settings\LocalService\Local Settings\Application Data\Micr
osoft\Windows\UsrClass.dat
0xe1be0008 0x0ef65008 \Device\HarddiskVolume1\Documents and Settings\LocalService\NTUSER.DAT
0xe1b86400 0x0e684400 \Device\HarddiskVolume1\Documents and Settings\NetworkService\Local Settings\Application Data\Mi
crosoft\Windows\UsrClass.dat
0xe1ba5008 0x0eb3b008 \Device\HarddiskVolume1\Documents and Settings\NetworkService\NTUSER.DAT
0xe1640b60 0x0a6e4b60 \Device\HarddiskVolume1\WINDOWS\system32\config\software
0xe162ab60 0x0a742b60 \Device\HarddiskVolume1\WINDOWS\system32\config\default
0xe16488d0 0x0a76f8d0 \Device\HarddiskVolume1\WINDOWS\system32\config\SECURITY
0xe171db60 0x04309b60 \Device\HarddiskVolume1\WINDOWS\system32\config\SAM
0xe140fb60 0x02e7cb60 [no name]
0xe1035b60 0x02a9eb60 \Device\HarddiskVolume1\WINDOWS\system32\config\system
0xe102e008 0x02a98008 [no name]
analyzer@volabox:~/Desktop$
```

Fig. 11.5 Volatility hivelist

```
analyzer@volabox:~/Desktop$ volatility -f testimg.vmem --profile="WinXPSP3x86" userassist
Volatility Foundation Volatility Framework 2.4
--------------------------
Registry: \Device\HarddiskVolume1\Documents and Settings\Administrator\NTUSER.DAT
Key name: Count
Last updated: 2011-01-06 14:37:41 UTC+0000

Subkeys:

Values:

REG_BINARY     UEME_CTLSESSION :
0x00000000  ee 34 5b 0e 04 00 00 00                              .4[.....

REG_BINARY     UEME_RUNPIDL:%csidl2%\MSN.lnk :
ID:            1
Count:        14
Last updated:  2010-08-22 17:36:30 UTC+0000
0x00000000  01 00 00 00 13 00 00 00 02 11 47 8e 20 42 cb 01   ..........G..B..
```

Fig. 11.6 Volatility userassist

that it has been used 14 times and the last update time should tell us when the item
was last used. Another interesting piece of information that can be extracted from
registry is the user's password hashes. As shown in Fig. 11.7, they can be dumped
using the *hashdump* module, which will also tell you the name and RID of each
user.

Looking at finding complete files in memory can begin with looking for MFT
records. Remember that small files can reside in the MFT. Dumping available MFT
records would be a way to dump those files. You can use the *mftparser* module to

```
analyzer@volabox:~/Desktop$ volatility -f testimg.vmem --profile="WinXPSP3x86" hashdump
Volatility Foundation Volatility Framework 2.4
Administrator:500:e52cac67419a9a224a3b108f3fa6cb6d:8846f7eaee8fb117ad06bdd830b7586c:::
Guest:501:aad3b435b51404eeaad3b435b51404ee:31d6cfe0d16ae931b73c59d7e0c089c0:::
HelpAssistant:1000:22d8685792cd2df8392f2d3ec8648d7e:bdedd3a3893c938a7fff9e4e1234f08a:::
SUPPORT_388945a0:1002:aad3b435b51404eeaad3b435b51404ee:4698b5e815592ec8a1a8d0073f04320b:::
ASPNET:1003:d451b674fa8c8dd8a1a050cb3180cd20:c1fa7ae2dd06c12186e44beaeea7bde8:::
analyzer@volabox:~/Desktop$
```

Fig. 11.7 Volatility hashdump

Fig. 11.8 Volatility mftparser

search for and dump MTF records, as shown in Fig. 11.8. Note that you need to supply an output directory. You can then use FTK to analyze the output in a structured way.

If you want to search further for files you can use the *filescan* module to search for files. Volatility also provides a module called *yarascan* that can be used for keyword or regular expression searches. By default, *yarascan* will return the search hit and some of the following data as well as the ID of the process owning the data. A sample *yarascan*, using a regular expression to search for URLs, is presented in Fig. 11.9.

One of the main reasons for analyzing memory, at least as presented in this book, is to find traces of encrypted data. Volatility provides three modules that can be used to find information relating to Truecrypt, a common encryption software. Those modules are:

- *Truecryptsummary* that returns a summary of information about Truecrypt
- *Truecryptpassphrase* that looks for cached Truecrypt passphrases
- *Truecryptmaster* that looks for Truecrypt master keys.

Figure 11.10 shows a usage example of *truecryptsummary*, in this case Truecrypt was not installed on the system and therefore the results are blank.

```
analyzer@volabox:~/Desktop$ volatility -f testimg.vmem --profile="WinXPSP3x86" yarascan -Y "/(www|http).+\.(com|net|org)/"
--wide [--kernel]
Volatility Foundation Volatility Framework 2.4
Rule: r1
Owner: Process csrss.exe Pid 636
0x00172080  68 00 74 00 74 00 70 00 3a 00 2f 00 2f 00 73 00   h.t.t.p.:./././.s.
0x00172090  63 00 68 00 65 00 6d 00 61 00 73 00 2e 00 6d 00   c.h.e.m.a.s...m.
0x001720a0  69 00 63 00 72 00 6f 00 73 00 6f 00 66 00 74 00   i.c.r.o.s.o.f.t.
0x001720b0  2e 00 63 00 6f 00 6d 00 2f 00 53 00 4d 00 49 00   ..c.o.m./.S.M.I.
0x001720c0  2f 00 32 00 30 00 30 00 35 00 2f 00 57 00 69 00   /.2.0.0.5./.W.i.
0x001720d0  6e 00 64 00 6f 00 77 00 73 00 53 00 65 00 74 00   n.d.o.w.s.S.e.t.
0x001720e0  74 00 69 00 6e 00 67 00 73 00 00 00 00 00 09 00   t.i.n.g.s.......
0x001720f0  08 00 31 00 90 01 08 00 d0 53 18 00 ad ad cb 01   ..1......S......
0x00172100  50 b6 16 00 90 af 16 00 60 bc 18 00 c0 87 b4 75   P.......`......u
0x00172110  cc 03 00 00 dc 04 00 00 c8 57 17 00 00 00 00 00   .........W......
0x00172120  e0 06 00 00 06 00 00 00 00 00 00 00 00 00 00 00   ................
0x00172130  08 00 08 00 a8 00 08 00 e8 db 18 00 e0 de 1a 00   ................
0x00172140  c8 24 17 00 a8 dd 1a 00 78 5a 18 00 20 87 b4 75   .$......xZ.....u
```

Fig. 11.9 Volatility yarascan

```
analyzer@volabox:~/Desktop$ volatility -f testimg.vmem --profile="WinXPSP3x86" truecryptsummary
Volatility Foundation Volatility Framework 2.4
analyzer@volabox:~/Desktop$
```

Fig. 11.10 Volatility truecryptsummary

```
analyzer@volabox:~/Desktop$ volatility -f testimg.vmem --profile="WinXPSP3x86" screenshot -D ~/Desktop/dump/
Volatility Foundation Volatility Framework 2.4
Wrote /home/analyzer/Desktop/dump/session_0.Service-0x0-3e7$.Default.png
Wrote /home/analyzer/Desktop/dump/session_0.Service-0x0-3e4$.Default.png
Wrote /home/analyzer/Desktop/dump/session_0.Service-0x0-3e5$.Default.png
Wrote /home/analyzer/Desktop/dump/session_0.SAWinSta.SADesktop.png
Wrote /home/analyzer/Desktop/dump/session_0.WinSta0.Default.png
Wrote /home/analyzer/Desktop/dump/session_0.WinSta0.Disconnect.png
Wrote /home/analyzer/Desktop/dump/session_0.WinSta0.Winlogon.png
analyzer@volabox:~/Desktop$
```

Fig. 11.11 Volatility screenshot

The final goodie that is displayed in this introduction to memory forensics is a rather cool module called *screenshot*, demonstrated in Fig. 11.11. What it returns is actually an attempt at a screenshot for every user that has an active session. While the results are not identical to a real screenshot it can provide an overview of what windows that was open on the computer at the time of the memory dump.

11.1 Questions and Tasks

The task for this chapter is for you to do a memory dump of you own computer and use volatility to try the discussed modules and examine the results.

References

Ligh, M. H., Case, A., Levy, J., & Walters, A. (2014). *The art of memory forensics: Detecting malware and threats in windows, linux, and Mac memory*. Wiley.
Volatility Foundation. (2017). Volatility Foundation. Available Online: http://www.volatilityfoundation.org/ [Fetched: 2017-07-06].

Part III
Vocabulary

This section is dedicated to explanations of words used throughout the book.

Chapter 12
Vocabulary

Abstract This chapter contains a short word list that describes some terms that are common within computer forensics.

Keywords Computer forensiscs · Vocabulary

Volatile data—The term volatile data refers to data that can quickly change or be lost. A common example of volatile data is the RAM memory. This is volatile because it is changed all the time and it is lost then the computer is powered off.

Forensic image—A forensically sound disk image is a bit-by-bit copy of a hard drive. To ensure that the evidence, which is the actual hard drive, is not modified or compromised a forensic examiner should make a disk image and investigate that. To ensure a forensically sound process a write blocker should be used when doing the disk image to ensure that no changes are made to the actual hard drive.

Physical image—A physical image is a disk image that is created by copying each bit on the hard drive, from beginning to end. A physical image is needed in order to make a complete search for data in slack space.

Logical image—A logical image is a copy of a live partition. In contrast to a physical image, it can be seen as a copy of a mounted partition and is commonly used to image encrypted drives. This is because, with a logical image, you get an image of the data ass seen by the operating system at the moment. For that reason, a logical image does not offer the opportunity to analyze slack space. It should only be used when a physical image is not possible, i.e., due to Full Disk Encryption.

Slack space—When a file is stored on a hard drive it is given a number of clusters on that drive. If it does not fully fill all allocated clusters the space from the end of the file to the end of the last allocated cluster may contain data previously stored on the hard drive. This space is called slack space.

Live examination—A live examination refers to an examination of a running system. Live forensics is another term that is commonly used with the same meaning as live examination.

J. Kävrestad, *Guide to Digital Forensics*, SpringerBriefs in Computer Science,
https://doi.org/10.1007/978-3-319-67450-6_12

Memory capture—Memory capture is the process of creating a memory dump. That is gathering the information in the internal memory (RAM) of a computer.

Write blocker—a write blocker is a physical device or software that prohibits a computer from writing any data to a disk. Since a computer will almost certainly write some data to a disk that is connected to it, write blockers are used in forensic examinations to prevent that.

Regular expression—regular expressions are used to express patterns that can, in example, be used to search through data.

Preprocessing—Preprocessing commonly refers to tasks that are completed in combination with setting up a case. In FTK, preprocessing is the tasks you choose to run at the case creation stage.

Port numbers—port numbers are used to address data to a certain service. Common services are associated with certain port numbers. For instance, SSH is associated with port 22. As such, a computer that wants to access another computer over SSH would address the port 22. Also, a firewall blocks or allows traffic based on port numbers. That makes the firewall rules a good source of information, if a port is open, the associated service is or has likely been installed.

Part IV
Appendices

Chapter 13
Appendix A—Solutions

Abstract This chapter lists answers to the review questions from each book chapter.

Keywords Computer forensics

This appendix presents answers to the questions and task for each chapter. Where it's not possible to provide an answer, a discussion is presented instead.

13.1 Chapter 1

1. Forensic experts are involved in almost every kind of case. It is very common for digital evidence to be present in any kind of investigation ranging from theft to fraud to murder. The forensic experts main duty is to examine digital evidence. The forensic expert may also assist during house searches and participate as a consultant on technical questions. It is quite common that the forensic expert is called to court as a witness and it happens that the forensic expert assists during interrogations.
2. In the example to investigate if someone broke company regulation. Forensic experts are commonly hired to analyze what happened during an intrusion or similar attack or to do recover data using forensic techniques.
3. All devices able to carry digital information.
4. The person who ordered the examination, the person owning or using the equipment that is being and examined and the justice system.

13.2 Chapter 2

What you should learn from this task is that digital evidence is common in almost all types of criminal cases. Discuss the results of this task with some of your peers and/or teacher!

© The Author(s) 2017
J. Kävrestad, *Guide to Digital Forensics*, SpringerBriefs in Computer Science,
https://doi.org/10.1007/978-3-319-67450-6_13

13.3   Chapter 3

1. Secondary storage devices are every type of device that can store digital information for long term preservation. While this excludes RAM and cache memory it includes all types of hard drives, USB sticks, flash cards, CD's, DVD's, tapes and more.
2. The file is removed from the MFT and thus, the drive space can be allocated to another file. Until the file is overwritten it can easily be recovered by searching for file signatures.
3. Resident files are completely located in MFT and non-resident files are not.
4. Because different applications store data in different ways.
5. Use Regedit to find out what time zone your computer is set to use.
6. A one-way function that takes some data as input and produces a digest that is unique for that input. For a hash algorithm to be secure it must be collision resistant and cannot be reversible.
7. It is much faster and can, therefore, crack longer passwords. However, it is quite weak against random passwords.

13.4   Chapter 4

1. Because memory holds information that shows what the computer has done since the last reboot. The memory can also hold valuable data such as passwords and encrypted versions of decrypted data.
2. It is a bit-by-bit copy of a storage device. It is considered best practice to create a disk image and analyze the disk image instead of the actual storage device during a forensic examination. This is to ensure that the storage device is not compromised.
3. Volatile data is data that is stored for short-term usage. The content of the RAM memory is an example of volatile data.
4. Preparation enhance the ability to perform a live examination with good results. One way to prepare is to have a pre-packed bag of tools, another way is to read up on the suspect that is targeted. This allows you to get an idea of what to expect on the scene.
5. It ensures that the computer that you are examining is not compromised and usually enhances performance.

13.5   Chapter 5

1. Unbiased means that the results are produced and presented in an objective manner and reproducible means that the way that the results were achieved is presented good enough for someone else to conduct the same examination with

the same results. In a criminal context, this is important to ensure a fair investigation and trial of the suspect of the crime.

2. a. Understand the case: Read up on the case to get an understanding of it
   b. Analyze questions/purpose: understand what the investigators want from the forensic examination
   c. Find basic information: Get basic information from the examined devices, such as users and registered owner
   d. Find information relating to objectives: Find data relating to what was established in (b)
   e. Analyze found information: Analyze the findings and draw conclusions
   f. Report: Present the findings to the investigators.

3. So that a reader can easily understand and interpret the conclusions drawn during the examination.

4. The simple answer is no in most legislation. This is because Dropbox is a cloud storage service. Analyzing data in the cloud will commonly require additional warrants.

13.6   Chapter 6

1. The images will likely differ in size since they were compressed in different ways.
2. You can use FTK imager, it is available for free from the Access Data web page.
3. You can use FTK imager, it is available for free from the Access Data web page.
4. The process is described by Halderman et al. (2009).

13.7   Chapter 7

1. The differences that appear are due to the fact that the index search is limited by settings for noise words, delimiters, and characters to include in the index. The live search will search all data in the case "as-is".
2. A common reason for why you are unsuccessful is that the authentication module of your operating system is not located in the lower 4 GB of RAM that inception can access. The reason can also be that your computer disables firmware ports when the login screen is shown.
3. Several free tools are available if you search for rar cracking. Using a dictionary with the password included should do the trick, a brute force is hard against a rar file as it uses a very slow encryption algorithm.

13.8   Chapter 8

1. Found in Windows registry
2. Found in Windows registry
3. Found in Windows registry
4. You can find this data by examining the MBR in FTK imager
5. Because the file itself is often not deleted. What is deleted is the entry in the MFT
6. A ZIP—archive is a compound file that needs to be expanded before it can be fully analyzed
7. EXIF data is metadata stored in pictures. Since it can include information such as GPS coordinates, model of the device taking the picture and name of the device taking the picture it is very interesting for a forensic examiner
8. Analyze the MBR to see if there are any gaps between the listed partitions. If gaps are found, the data in the gaps should be further examined to look for signatures of partitions.

13.9   Chapter 9

Discuss the results of this task with some of your peers and/or teacher!

13.10   Chapter 11

Discuss the results of this task with some of your peers and/or teacher!

Reference

Halderman, J. A., Schoen, S. D., Heninger, N., Clarkson, W., Paul, W., Calandrino, J. A., et al. (2009). Lest we remember: Cold-boot attacks on encryption keys. *Communications of the ACM, 52*(5), 91–98.

Chapter 14
Appendix B—Useful Scripts

Abstract This chapter presents the source code of scripts that can be used during live investigations to collects some basic data. there is one script for Windows and one for Linux. There is also a script used to parse jitsi chat logs.

Keywords Forensic scripting · Computer forensics · Live forensics

This appendix lists a couple of scripts that can be useful for computer forensic experts. Feel free to use, modify, and redistribute as you want and need.

14.1 Capturing Basic Computer Information on MAC and Linux

```
#!/usr/bin/perl
use warnings;
use strict;

#Script that gathers computer time setting and IP-configuration from
running MAC/Linux system
#NOTE: Designed and tested for MAC OS X
print ``NOTE! Run the script with elevated permissions if possible (i.e. as
root of with sudo)\n'';

print ``chose name of output file (Will be stored in the location the script
is ran from)\n'';
my $outputname = <>;
chomp($outputname);
open(OUT, `` ≫'' ,``$outputname\.txt'') or die ``Cant open output file'';

print ``do you want to add case data to outputfile? (yes/no)\n'';
my $i = <>;
```

```perl
chomp ($i);
if($i = ~/yes/){
        print OUT ``—Case data—\n\n'';
        print ``submit case number:'';
        my $casenumber = <>;
        print OUT ``CASE: $casenumber'';

        print ``\nsubmit evidence number:'';
        my $evidence = <>;
        print OUT ``EVIDENCE: $evidence'';

        print ``\nsubmit examiner name:'';
        my $name = <>;
        print OUT ``EXAMINER: $name'';
        print ``\nsubmit current date and time (Fröken UR):'';
        my $realtime = <>;
        print OUT ``Time of examination: $realtime'';
        print OUT ``\n\n—Gathered data presented below—\n'';
        }

print ``\nGathering date and time.......\n'';

use POSIX qw(strftime);
my $date = strftime ``%Y%m%d_%H%M'', localtime;
print OUT ``####System date and time###\n $date\n\n'';

print ``Gathering system hostname......\n'';

my $hostname = 'hostname';

print OUT ``####System hostname (including domain information if present)
####\n $hostname\n'';

print ``Gathering system IP-configuration......\n'';
my $IPinfo = 'ifconfig';
print OUT ``####System ip configuration####\n $IPinfo\n\n'';

print ``Gathering list of open connections (UDP/TCP)......\n'';
my $OC = 'netstat -ant';
my @OC = split(/Active LOCAL/,$OC);

print OUT ``####List of open connections####\n $OC[0]\n\n'';
```

```perl
print ``Gathering list of running processes......\n'';
my $processes = 'ps -ef';
print OUT ``####List of running processes####\n $processes\n\n'';


print ``Gathering list of mounted drives/shares......\n'';
my $mounts = 'mount';
print OUT ``####List of mounted drives/shares####\n $mounts\n\n'';


print ``Gathering list of system users......\n'';
print OUT ``####Information about system users####\n '';
my @users = 'dscl \. list /Users | grep -v ^_\.\*';
foreach (@users) {
        my $info = 'id $_';
        chomp($_);
        print OUT ``\n-Information about the user $_ -\n'';
        print OUT $info;
}
close (OUT);
```


14.2   Capturing Basic Computer Information on Windows


```powershell
#Script that gathers computer time setting and IP-configuration from running
Windows
#Note that the script is designed for minimum memory usage
$outpath = Read-host -Prompt 'This script gather basic computer informa-
tion. Input full path to the output file: '

[Datetime]::Now | Out-File -Append $outpath
Get-WmiObject Win32_Computersystem | Out-File -Append $outpath
get-wmiobject win32_networkadapterconfiguration -filter ``ipenabled =
true'' | Out-File -Append $outpath
netstat -aonp TCP| Out-File -Append $outpath
Get-Process| Out-File -Append $outpath
gwmi -Class Win32_LogicalDisk| Out-File -Append $outpath
Get-WmiObject -Class Win32_UserAccount -Filter ``LocalAccount = 'True'''|
Out-File -Append $outpath
```

14.3   Parse Jitsi Chat Logs

```
#Script that parses jitsi chat logs and prints in a nice format.
#Note < msg > section needs to be cleaned to only include < msg > MESSAGE </msg
> before #usnig the script
#This can be done using search and replace in some text editor
#Promt for input and output file paths and username of the local and remote
chat #accounts
$path = Read-Host ``Enter path to source file: ''
$outpath = Read-Host ``Enter path, including filename, to output file: ''
$local = Read-Host ``Enter the local username: ''
$remote = Read-Host ``Enter remote username: ''

#Initiate arrays used later
$messages = @()
$messages_tidy = @()

#Import chat log content into a XML object, then select specific objects of
interest
[xml]$chatlog = Get-Content $path
$chatlog.history.record | %{$messages += $_.dir + ``;'' + $_.msg + ``;'' +
$_.timestamp}

#Replace in and out keywords width actual usernames
foreach($index in $messages){
  if($index -like ``out*''){

    [regex]$pattern = ``out''
    $messages_tidy += $pattern.replace($index,$local, 1)
    }
  elseif($index -like ``in*''){
    [regex]$pattern = ``in''
    $messages_tidy += $pattern.replace($index, $remote, 1)
    }
  }
```

Chapter 15
Appendix C—Sample Report Template

Abstract This chapter presents a sample report template that can be used to report forensic examinations.

Keywords Reporting · Computer forensiscs · Forensic report

Sample police station	Date of examination	Case number
Forensics dept. of Bergen	2017-05-17	3443-1231-17
Address		

Protocol of forensic examination of computer 1234567-32

15.1 Examination Data

Examination requested by:	Name of requesting officer
Lead forensic investigator:	Name of forensic expert in charge
Reason for examination:	Questions and objectives
Time of examination	Timespan of the examination
Additional information	Additional information such as what the suspect or some other person claimed.

15.1.1 Summary

Provide a short summary of the examination and the results. It can be clever to include a vocabulary at the end of the report and mark all words explained in the vocabulary, for instance using a "*". Refer to the vocabulary in the summary. If the

J. Kävrestad, *Guide to Digital Forensics*, SpringerBriefs in Computer Science,
https://doi.org/10.1007/978-3-319-67450-6_15

examination covers one piece of evidence you can note the evidence identified in the headline, otherwise, you need to list all evidence covered in the report, for instance, with a listing in the summary*.

15.1.2   Findings

Your report should include a chapter with your objective findings. Whenever appropriate, include how you uncovered your findings and refer to exported material. A good line would be: Pictures that appear to be of pills was found on the desktop, they were exported and delivered to the investigator on a USB drive. Further, GPS coordinates (1234, 1234) and model name (Canon D105) of the camera taking the picture was found in the metadata of all pictures.

15.2   Conclusions

The conclusions section is where you can draw a conclusion based on your findings. You may also include other sources of data such as information from interrogations or likewise. Based on the sample findings above a proper line could be: A visual inspections of the encountered pictured tells that they seem to be of pills similar to the drugs seized during the house search. Further, the GPS coordinated matches the suspect's home address and a camera used to take the pictures was the same as the one found in the suspect's home. In conclusion, the analysis strongly suggests that the pictures were taken at the suspect's home address and portraits the same or similar pills as the ones found during the house search.

15.2.1   Word List

Summary—a summary is a short version of something.
   Joakim Kävrestad.
   Forensic examiner at some police department.

Chapter 16
Appendix D—List of Time Zones

Abstract This chapter contains a table of time zones used in Windows systems.

Keywords Timezones · Computer forensiscs

See Table 16.1.

Table 16.1 List of Time zones (Microsoft 2017-3)

Name of time zone	Time
Dateline Standard Time	(GMT-12:00) International Date Line West
Samoa Standard Time	(GMT-11:00) Midway Island, Samoa
Hawaiian Standard Time	(GMT-10:00) Hawaii
Alaskan Standard Time	(GMT-09:00) Alaska
Pacific Standard Time	(GMT-08:00) Pacific Time (US and Canada); Tijuana
Mountain Standard Time	(GMT-07:00) Mountain Time (US and Canada)
Mexico Standard Time 2	(GMT-07:00) Chihuahua, La Paz, Mazatlan
U.S. Mountain Standard Time	(GMT-07:00) Arizona
Central Standard Time	(GMT-06:00) Central Time (US and Canada
Canada Central Standard Time	(GMT-06:00) Saskatchewan
Mexico Standard Time	(GMT-06:00) Guadalajara, Mexico City, Monterrey
Central America Standard Time	(GMT-06:00) Central America
Eastern Standard Time	(GMT-05:00) Eastern Time (US and Canada)
U.S. Eastern Standard Time	(GMT-05:00) Indiana (East)
S.A. Pacific Standard Time	(GMT-05:00) Bogota, Lima, Quito
Atlantic Standard Time	(GMT-04:00) Atlantic Time (Canada)
S.A. Western Standard Time	(GMT-04:00) Caracas, La Paz
Pacific S.A. Standard Time	(GMT-04:00) Santiago
Newfoundland and Labrador Standard Time	(GMT-03:30) Newfoundland and Labrador

(continued)

© The Author(s) 2017
J. Kävrestad, *Guide to Digital Forensics*, SpringerBriefs in Computer Science,
https://doi.org/10.1007/978-3-319-67450-6_16

Table 16.1 (continued)

Name of time zone	Time
E. South America Standard Time	(GMT-03:00) Brasilia
S.A. Eastern Standard Time	(GMT-03:00) Buenos Aires, Georgetown
Greenland Standard Time	(GMT-03:00) Greenland
Mid-Atlantic Standard Time	(GMT-02:00) Mid-Atlantic
Azores Standard Time	(GMT-01:00) Azores
Cape Verde Standard Time	(GMT-01:00) Cape Verde Islands
GMT Standard Time	(GMT) Greenwich Mean Time: Dublin, Edinburgh, Lisbon, London
Greenwich Standard Time	(GMT) Casablanca, Monrovia
Central Europe Standard Time	(GMT+01:00) Belgrade, Bratislava, Budapest, Ljubljana, Prague
Central European Standard Time	(GMT+01:00) Sarajevo, Skopje, Warsaw, Zagreb
Romance Standard Time	(GMT+01:00) Brussels, Copenhagen, Madrid, Paris
W. Europe Standard Time	(GMT+01:00) Amsterdam, Berlin, Bern, Rome, Stockholm, Vienna
W. Central Africa Standard Time	(GMT+01:00) West Central Africa
E. Europe Standard Time	(GMT+02:00) Bucharest
Egypt Standard Time	(GMT+02:00) Cairo
FLE Standard Time	(GMT+02:00) Helsinki, Kiev, Riga, Sofia, Tallinn, Vilnius
GTB Standard Time	(GMT+02:00) Athens, Istanbul, Minsk
Israel Standard Time	(GMT+02:00) Jerusalem
South Africa Standard Time	(GMT+02:00) Harare, Pretoria
Russian Standard Time	(GMT+03:00) Moscow, St. Petersburg, Volgograd
Arab Standard Time	(GMT+03:00) Kuwait, Riyadh
E. Africa Standard Time	(GMT+03:00) Nairobi
Arabic Standard Time	(GMT+03:00) Baghdad
Iran Standard Time	(GMT+03:30) Tehran
Arabian Standard Time	(GMT+04:00) Abu Dhabi, Muscat
Caucasus Standard Time	(GMT+04:00) Baku, Tbilisi, Yerevan
Transitional Islamic State of Afghanistan Standard Time	(GMT+04:30) Kabul
Ekaterinburg Standard Time	(GMT+05:00) Ekaterinburg
West Asia Standard Time	(GMT+05:00) Islamabad, Karachi, Tashkent
India Standard Time	(GMT+05:30) Chennai, Kolkata, Mumbai, New Delhi
Nepal Standard Time	(GMT+05:45) Kathmandu
Central Asia Standard Time	(GMT+06:00) Astana, Dhaka

(continued)

Table 16.1 (continued)

Name of time zone	Time
Sri Lanka Standard Time	(GMT+06:00) Sri Jayawardenepura
N. Central Asia Standard Time	(GMT+06:00) Almaty, Novosibirsk
Myanmar Standard Time	(GMT+06:30) Yangon Rangoon
S.E. Asia Standard Time	(GMT+07:00) Bangkok, Hanoi, Jakarta
North Asia Standard Time	(GMT+07:00) Krasnoyarsk
China Standard Time	(GMT+08:00) Beijing, Chongqing, Hong Kong SAR, Urumqi
Singapore Standard Time	(GMT+08:00) Kuala Lumpur, Singapore
Taipei Standard Time	(GMT+08:00) Taipei
W. Australia Standard Time	(GMT+08:00) Perth
North Asia East Standard Time	(GMT+08:00) Irkutsk, Ulaanbaatar
Korea Standard Time	(GMT+09:00) Seoul
Tokyo Standard Time	(GMT+09:00) Osaka, Sapporo, Tokyo
Yakutsk Standard Time	(GMT+09:00) Yakutsk
A.U.S. Central Standard Time	(GMT+09:30) Darwin
Cen. Australia Standard Time	(GMT+09:30) Adelaide
A.U.S. Eastern Standard Time	(GMT+10:00) Canberra, Melbourne, Sydney
E. Australia Standard Time	(GMT+10:00) Brisbane
Tasmania Standard Time	(GMT+10:00) Hobart
Vladivostok Standard Time	(GMT+10:00) Vladivostok
West Pacific Standard Time	(GMT+10:00) Guam, Port Moresby
Central Pacific Standard Time	(GMT+11:00) Magadan, Solomon Islands, New Caledonia
Fiji Islands Standard Time	(GMT+12:00) Fiji Islands, Kamchatka, Marshall Islands
New Zealand Standard Time	(GMT+12:00) Auckland, Wellington
Tonga Standard Time	(GMT+13:00) Nuku'alofa

Reference

Microsoft. (2017-3). Microsoft time zone index values. Available online: https://msdn.microsoft.com/en-us/library/ms912391(v=winembedded.11).aspx [Fetched: 2017-07-01].

Chapter 17
Appendix E—Complete Jitsi Chat Log

Abstract This chapter presents a chat log extracted from the chat client jitsi.

Keywords Jitsi · Chat log · Computer forensics

```
<?xml version=``1.0'' encoding=``UTF-8'' standalone=``no''?>
<history>
    <record timestamp=``2017-06-27T13:16:07.826+0200''>
        <dir>in</dir>
        <msg><![CDATA[zup_]]></msg>
        <msgTyp>text/plain</msgTyp>
        <enc>UTF-8</enc>
        <uid>149856217370418137890</uid>
  <receivedTimestamp>2017-06-27T13:16:07.260+0200</receivedTimestamp>
    </record>
    <record timestamp=``201 7-06-27T13:16:21.179+0200''>
        <dir>out</dir>
        <msg><![CDATA[kollar lite affärer....sj?]]></msg>
        <msgTyp>text/plain</msgTyp>
        <enc>UTF-8</enc>
        <uid>149856218114519064878</uid>
  <receivedTimestamp>2017-06-27T13:16:21.149+0200</receivedTimestamp>
    </record>
    <record timestamp=``2017-06-27T13:16:42.293+0200''>
        <dir>in</dir>
      <msg><![CDATA[samma, lurar p[ vad som ar vart att salja..]]></msg>
        <msgTyp>text/plain</msgTyp>
        <enc>UTF-8</enc>
        <uid>149856220870413141993</uid>
  <receivedTimestamp>2017-06-27T13:16:42.259+0200</receivedTimestamp>
    </record>
```

© The Author(s) 2017

J. Kävrestad, *Guide to Digital Forensics*, SpringerBriefs in Computer Science,
https://doi.org/10.1007/978-3-319-67450-6_17

```
    <record timestamp=``2017-06-27T13:16:52.792+0200''>
       <dir>out</dir>
       <msg><![CDATA[hur säkrar du?]]></msg>
       <msgTyp>text/plain</msgTyp>
       <enc>UTF-8</enc>
       <uid>149856221278425383895</uid>
<receivedTimestamp>2017-06-27T13:16:52.785+0200</receivedTimestamp>
    </record>
    <record timestamp=``2017-06-27T13:17:20.785+0200''>
       <dir>in</dir>
<msg><![CDATA[kor engelsk dator, svart lista ut vart jag ar!]]></msg>
       <msgTyp>text/plain</msgTyp>
       <enc>UTF-8</enc>
       <uid>149856224722021689995</uid>
<receivedTimestamp>2017-06-27T13:17:20.774+0200</receivedTimestamp>
    </record>
    <record timestamp=``2017-06-27T13:17:30.963+0200''>
       <dir>out</dir>
       <msg><![CDATA[tror inte det funkar, ,lira tor!]]></msg>
       <msgTyp>text/plain</msgTyp>
       <enc>UTF-8</enc>
       <uid>149856225095331490715</uid>
<receivedTimestamp>2017-06-27T13:17:30.955+0200</receivedTimestamp>
    </record>
    <record timestamp=``2017-06-27T13:17:46.289+0200''>
       <dir>in</dir>
       <msg><![CDATA[har kollat pa det, vet inte, krangligt!]]></msg>
       <msgTyp>text/plain</msgTyp>
       <enc>UTF-8</enc>
       <uid>14985622727203437744</uid>
<receivedTimestamp>2017-06-27T13:17:46.272+0200</receivedTimestamp>
    </record>
    <record timestamp=``2017-06-27T13:18:16.749+0200''>
       <dir>out</dir>
       <msg><![CDATA[vi får se...., ska ut o köra nu]]></msg>
       <msgTyp>text/plain</msgTyp>
       <enc>UTF-8</enc>
       <uid>14985622967401999847</uid>
<receivedTimestamp>2017-06-27T13:18:16.741+0200</receivedTimestamp>
    </record>
    <record timestamp=``2017-06-27T13:18:22.691+0200''>
       <dir>in</dir>
       <msg><![CDATA[k thx bye]]></msg>
       <msgTyp>text/plain</msgTyp>
       <enc>UTF-8</enc>
```

```
         <uid>14985623091289998450</uid>
  <receivedTimestamp>2017-06-27T13:18:22.680+0200</receivedTimestamp>
    </record>
<record timestamp=``2017-06-29T09:25:10.619+0200''>
         <dir>in</dir>
         <msg><![CDATA[hade din konakt winky eller?]]></msg>
         <msgTyp>text/plain</msgTyp>
         <enc>UTF-8</enc>
         <uid>14987211183323157419</uid>
  <receivedTimestamp>2017-06-29T09:25:10.584+0200</receivedTimestamp>
    </record>
    <record timestamp=``2017-06-29T09:25:16.007+0200''>
         <dir>out</dir>
         <msg><![CDATA[ring]]></msg>
         <msgTyp>text/plain</msgTyp>
         <enc>UTF-8</enc>
         <uid>14987211160015132863</uid>
  <receivedTimestamp>2017-06-29T09:25:16.003+0200</receivedTimestamp>
    </record>
<record timestamp=``2017-06-29T11:28:56.442+0200''>
         <dir>in</dir>
 <msg><![CDATA[lol, din gubbe ville att jag ska betala till polen, tror du
detta funkar för att göra bakkoton?]]></msg>
         <msgTyp>text/plain</msgTyp>
         <enc>UTF-8</enc>
         <uid>14987285280463335586</uid>
  <receivedTimestamp>2017-06-29T11:29:00.000+0200</receivedTimestamp>
    </record>
    <record timestamp=``2017-06-29T11:29:19.585+0200''>
         <dir>out</dir>
         <msg><![CDATA[hallå SKICKA INTE SÅNT!]]></msg>
         <msgTyp>text/plain</msgTyp>
         <enc>UTF-8</enc>
         <uid>14987285595673328 9131</uid>
  <receivedTimestamp>2017-06-29T11:29:19.576+0200</receivedTimestamp>
    </record>
    <record timestamp=``2017-06-29T11:29:28.633+0200''>
         <dir>out</dir>
         <msg><![CDATA[men ja.....idiot!]]></msg>
         <msgTyp>text/plain</msgTyp>
         <enc>UTF-8</enc>
         <uid>14987285686221 4632876</uid>
  <receivedTimestamp>2017-06-29T11:29:28.625+0200</receivedTimestamp>
    </record>
    <record timestamp=``2017-06-29T11:29:38.044+0200''>
```

```
        <dir>out</dir>
        <msg><![CDATA[lugn, jag shreddar den]]></msg>
        <msgTyp>text/plain</msgTyp>
        <enc>UTF-8</enc>
        <uid>14987285780318102467</uid>
 <receivedTimestamp>2017-06-29T11:29:38.034+0200</receivedTimestamp>
    </record>
    <record timestamp=``2017-06-29T11:30:13.642+0200''>
        <dir>in</dir>
        <msg><![CDATA[rätt najs väder hos hemma!]]></msg>
        <msgTyp>text/plain</msgTyp>
        <enc>UTF-8</enc>
        <uid>14987286112643 0554666</uid>
 <receivedTimestamp>2017-06-29T11:30:13.633+0200</receivedTimestamp>
    </record>
    <record timestamp=``2017-06-29T11:31:09.292+0200''>
        <dir>out</dir>
        <msg><![CDATA[gött, ordning på saker?]]></msg>
        <msgTyp>text/plain</msgTyp>
        <enc>UTF-8</enc>
        <uid>14987286692808427856</uid>
 <receivedTimestamp>2017-06-29T11:31:09.284+0200</receivedTimestamp>
    </record>
    <record timestamp=``2017-06-29T11:31:18.105+0200''>
        <dir>in</dir>
        <msg><![CDATA[visst, rullar på karnekegränd!]]></msg>
        <msgTyp>text/plain</msgTyp>
        <enc>UTF-8</enc>
        <uid>14987286757172 9818420</uid>
 <receivedTimestamp>2017-06-29T11:31:18.096+0200</receivedTimestamp>
    </record>
    <record timestamp=``2017-06-29T11:31:28.658+0200''>
        <dir>out</dir>
        <msg><![CDATA[kasnke vi ska slå samman?]]></msg>
        <msgTyp>text/plain</msgTyp>
        <enc>UTF-8</enc>
        <uid>14987286886433 1461466</uid>
 <receivedTimestamp>2017-06-29T11:31:28.648+0200</receivedTimestamp>
    </record>
    <record timestamp=``2017-06-29T11:31:40.794+0200''>
        <dir>in</dir>
        <msg><![CDATA[får se, bra o ha ensam buisness]]></msg>
        <msgTyp>text/plain</msgTyp>
        <enc>UTF-8</enc>
        <uid>14987286984212875993</uid>
```

```
    <receivedTimestamp>2017-06-29T11:31:40.786+0200</receivedTimestamp>
    </record>
    <record timestamp=``2017-06-29T11:43:25.330+0200''>
        <dir>in</dir>
<msg><![CDATA[lol på bilerna på dig me mina saker...ser ganster ut]]></msg>
        <msgTyp>text/plain</msgTyp>
        <enc>UTF-8</enc>
        <uid>149872940290527785517</uid>
  <receivedTimestamp>2017-06-29T11:43:25.322+0200</receivedTimestamp>
    </record>
    <record timestamp=``2017-06-29T11:43:45.855+0200''>
        <dir>out</dir>
<msg><![CDATA[haha idd, du hade av metadata på kameran va?]]></msg>
        <msgTyp>text/plain</msgTyp>
        <enc>UTF-8</enc>
        <uid>149872942584328989997</uid>
  <receivedTimestamp>2017-06-29T11:43:45.847+0200</receivedTimestamp>
    </record>
    <record timestamp=``2017-06-29T11:43:55.456+0200''>
        <dir>in</dir>
        <msg><![CDATA[lol ja e la inte dum eller, altid AV1]]></msg>
        <msgTyp>text/plain</msgTyp>
        <enc>UTF-8</enc>
        <uid>149872943303024228041</uid>
  <receivedTimestamp>2017-06-29T11:43:55.448+0200</receivedTimestamp>
    </record>
    <record timestamp=``2017-06-30T10:07:32.788+0200''>
        <dir>in</dir>
        <msg><![CDATA[fixa mer winks]]></msg>
        <msgTyp>text/plain</msgTyp>
        <enc>UTF-8</enc>
        <uid>149881004661110933177</uid>
  <receivedTimestamp>2017-06-30T10:07:32.777+0200</receivedTimestamp>
    </record>
    <record timestamp=``2017-06-30T10:07:38.409+0200''>
        <dir>out</dir>
        <msg><![CDATA[kom fort]]></msg>
        <msgTyp>text/plain</msgTyp>
        <enc>UTF-8</enc>
        <uid>149881005839726360958</uid>
  <receivedTimestamp>2017-06-30T10:07:38.398+0200</receivedTimestamp>
    </record>
</history>
```

Printed in the United States
By Bookmasters